T0279742

Mother *to* Mother

Mother *to* Mother

Spiritual and Practical Wisdom from the Cloister to the Home

Mary Elizabeth Cuff, PhD

TAN Books
Gastonia, North Carolina

Cover design by Caroline Green

Cover image: Maternity, 1917 (oil on canvas), Leighton, Edmund Blair, Photo © Christie's Images / Bridgeman Images

Library of Congress Control Number: 2024932562

ISBN: 978-1-5051-3027-0
Kindle ISBN: 978-1-5051-3012-6
ePUB ISBN: 978-1-5051-3013-3

Published in the United States by
TAN Books
PO Box 269
Gastonia, NC 28053
www.TANBooks.com

Printed in the United States of America

To my mother, whose selfless dedication to the vocation of motherhood was, is, and will continue to be my best inspiration.

Contents

Introduction

"O pure and virgin Lady, O spotless Theotokos:
Rejoice, O unwedded Bride!

O Virgin Queen and Mother, O dewey fleece
most sacred: Rejoice, O unwedded Bride!

O height transcending heaven above, O beam of
light most radiant: Rejoice O unwedded Bride!

O joy of chaste and virgin maids, surpassing all
the angels: Rejoice O unwedded Bride!"

—from the hymn "O Pure Virgin" by Nectarios of Aegina

On a crisp autumn day, a bunch of women from my Catholic mothers' group were standing around one of our favorite meet-up spots, chatting while our kids whizzed around in the excitement of imaginative play. Suddenly, into the midst of this very ordinary playdate, strolled a Capuchin nun. She was the sister-in-law of one of the moms, home for a brief visit. I had recently published an article about the ongoing crisis of monastic life in the Church, so the two of us fell to talking about various reasons why many female monastic communities struggle to attract vocations. We agreed that modern people, even many faithful Catholics, have difficulty imagining the life of a contemplative nun. Because these nuns live a life hidden away, it is easy to slip into the idea that they are completely detached from the rest of us and really have nothing to do with the world at all.

This is a particular issue for a contemplative monastic. Everyone loves nuns from the active orders who teach in schools, visit prisoners, or work as nurses. We can see them in action, and we know how—at least on the visible level—they fit into the larger world that we also know and occupy. They, for all their differences, have something that looks a bit like a career, so we know what sort of rubrics by which we can imagine part of their lives.

Cloistered and contemplative nuns, on the other hand . . . well, so many of us have no idea what they get up to in those monasteries all day long. It is difficult to shake the idea that they must levitate or spend all hours in the chapel on their knees. They might as well be from the Middle Ages, or live on the moon, for all we know about their world. "But really," the nun at the playground said with a laugh, looking at all of us, "contemplative nuns are the stay-at-home moms of the religious vocation!"

The parallel struck me like a thunderclap. Just like the life of a cloistered nun, there is so much ignorance, fear, and dismissiveness about the life of a stay-at-home mother. When a friend of mine joined a convent, well-meaning people, even in her own family, could not help voicing their worry that she was wasting her talents and education. This was about the same time that another friend of mine "got married too young" by her own parents' estimation. Her parents were distraught by her plan to have a large family. They had hoped she would focus on her promising career and "get established" before pausing for motherhood down the road.

And then there is the similarity in the outside world's attitude about what it is we do all day. Contemplative nuns are not shut-ins who have fled from all the world's problems, nor are they oppressed women who need reformers to liberate them from their rules and enclosed walls. In fact, if you look at the history of many old religious orders, it is the nuns themselves who fought for their veils, their cloisters, and their charisms. Many of them carry on that fight today, in the face of a world—and sometimes even a Church—that does not understand why they want it all.

Similarly, many moms do not spend the whole day "babysitting" our own children, sighing after better government programs to liberate us from the "burden of childcare." Those of us blessed with the privilege to stay home with our children are not victims of the so-called patriarchy. The fact of the matter is: both nuns, contemplative or active, and mothers, stay-at-home or working, spend a good deal of time doing vitally important work that no dollar amount could replace and nobody else could do. In other words, both nuns and moms are called to that sacred task of *motherhood*.

In his magnificent analysis of the modern family and the Church, *Familiaris Consortio*, Pope Saint John Paul

II emphasized the deep harmony that exists between the religious and married vocations. While the world might look at a nun and a mom and see two women who have chosen opposite lives, the pope explains that "virginity or celibacy for the sake of the Kingdom of God not only does not contradict the dignity of marriage but presupposes it and confirms it. Marriage and virginity or celibacy are two ways of expressing and living the one mystery of the covenant of God with His people."[1]

In other words, the lay mother with her children and the mother superior with her religious daughters are all walking in the same direction, their eyes on the same prize and their hearts pulled by the same desire. It is not a coincidence that the Church calls both of them *mother* and enshrines their vocations by means of vows not meant to be broken.

Amazingly, such is God's beautiful plan for his children that, at the end of the day, the two vocations mystically become the same. Pope Saint John Paul II explains it better than I ever could: "in spite of having renounced physical fecundity, the celibate person becomes spiritually fruitful, the father and mother of many, cooperating in the realization of the family according to God's plan."[2] The enduring reality of God's covenant is that it is always about family. The hermit alone in the desert, the homeschool mom who

---

[1]   John Paul II, *Familiaris Consortio*. https://www.vatican.va f/content/john-paul-ii/en/apost_exhortations/documents/hf_jp-ii _exh_19811122_familiaris-consortio.html.

[2]   John Paul II, *Familiaris Consortio*.

never manages to find a moment alone, and everyone in between are all part of this beautiful reality: that God wills all of us to be part of His family. And because of that, we are all called to be mothers or fathers, in imitation of God our father and Mary our mother.

And that is the other connection between the contemplative nun and the mother: both of us can look to Our Lady as the perfect model of our own particular vocation. Mary is both the virgin, pondering God in the quiet cloister of her heart, and the *Theotokos*: the literal, physical Mother of God. As the virgin, Mary is the original and best nun, wrapped in contemplation of the presence of God. As the *Theotokos*, she is also the greatest mother, raising her divine son according to the majestic plans of God. She shows all of us women how best to live out each ancient vocation which the Church has offered us: the religious life of a nun and the married life of a mother.

While mothers and nuns both have Our Lady as our perfect role model, most of us often seek out the perspective of others in our own respective vocations. I am sure that mothers have been asking other mothers for advice since Eve got a daughter-in-law, but these days, when being a Christian mother is often seen as being counter-cultural, the support and perspective of fellow mothers is even more essential for many of us. I know I have benefitted from the wisdom and knowledge of my own mother, my mother-in-law, and the mothers in my own community. But what about asking the mothers in the other vocation for advice? After all, as religious mothers, they have a unique perspective on our common call to motherhood.

Father John Hardon, SJ, the founder of the Institute for Religious Life, commented that, while there are exceptions that prove the rule, successful religious vocations by and large come from strong Catholic families that have provided good soil for their children's budding vocations.[3] Most monastics, therefore, have directly benefited from the nurturing influence of the married vocation through their parents. But it is a rare Catholic laywoman who knows a contemplative nun and can benefit from her insights and wisdom. Therefore, this book offers lay mothers the chance to meet and learn from mother superiors and nuns from five different monastic communities. These religious women have graciously shared their perspectives on common struggles and situations that confront both contemplative nuns and lay mothers.

This book is not just for one type of mother or stage of motherhood. I am writing from the perspective of a stay-at-home homeschool mom, but in the past, I wore the hat of a working mom in academia. The topics I have gathered are inspired by conversations with moms of all stripes who jumped at the opportunity to hear the insight of a contemplative nun about a struggle or concern close

---

[3]   See Fr. John Harden, *The Catholic Family and Vocations.* http://www.therealpresence.org/archives/Family/Family_014.htm.

to their heart. I hope that you find the nuns' reflections as moving and inspirational as I found them.

Therefore, the book is not necessarily best read from cover to cover (though you can do that, too!). Rather than large chapters that might require more time and focus than you can manage right now, the book is organized by small topics that contain several related questions and respective answered reflections by one or more of the nuns who helped me with the book. Feel free to jump around and pick sections that might be close to your heart at the moment. Each individual topic is short enough to allow for a relatively quick read if you, like me, read in the tiny fragments of time you find in the corners of your day.

There are five contemplative monasteries who graciously offered their insights for this book. I would like to take a few pages to introduce you to these delightful religious women and their monastic communities. Just like lay mothers, these religious are unique from each other, with different charisms, styles, and emphases based upon the distinctives of their orders. Yet they are also very similar: they take their vocational calling deeply seriously and seek to answer the summons to spiritual motherhood. They seek to model our Mother Mary in their lives for the sake of the Church. Pray for many vocations to their orders and to all faithful religious communities. They pray for all of us wives, mothers, and families.

Woman's destiny is love. When she is loved, she is most completely herself, able to expand and unfold the riches of her being as a flower opens its full beauty only in sunlight. When she loves, she is exercising her great mission in life. And if love is the life work of all women, it is the particular vocation of the contemplative religious woman.[4]

---

[4]   Mother Mary Francis, *Strange Gods Before Me,* Poor Clare Monastery of Our Lady of Guadalupe. Republished via Blurb, Incorporated, 2021. 85.

CHAPTER 1

Monasteries

The Poor Clare Monastery of Our Lady of Guadalupe in Roswell, New Mexico

Mother Mary Angela is the abbess of the Poor Clare Monastery of Our Lady of Guadalupe in Roswell, New Mexico. There are currently twenty-five of Saint Francis's Poor Ladies in the Roswell community, which has graced the New Mexico desert since 1948, when a group of Poor Clares from Chicago settled into an old farmhouse at the invitation of the bishop—who worried over the spiritual well-being of his "least Catholic" city. God has smiled on the faithful nuns in Roswell, who have been blessed with so many vocations over the years that they have founded six daughter monasteries across the world.

The Roswell contemplative Poor Clares seek to live out their charism to be a scriptural people by many customs woven into their monastic life. These customs have been handed down through the centuries and find their origin in the Rule of Saint Francis: "to observe the holy Gospel of our Lord Jesus Christ, by living in obedience, without anything of our own, and in chastity."[5] As contemplative Poor Clares, the nuns practice radical poverty within the confines of papal enclosure, which is the strictest form of cloistered monastic life, and which characterized the traditional Poor Clare life since the beginning of the order. Their habits are cut in the exact style of their saintly foundress: a rough gray-brown habit in the shape of a cross, the hem of which they often kiss because it is a sign of their consecration to God.

As a scriptural people, the Poor Clares take seriously their call to fulfill Christ's articulation of family: "For whoever does the will of my Father in heaven is my brother, and sister, and mother."[6] The nuns call each other sister because they are called both to be Christ for each other and to seek out Christ in each other. They are thus sisters and mothers in Christ. Their saintly founder, Francis himself, commented on the concept of being Christ's mother: "he tells us that receiving the word of God in our heart, we 'through love and a pure and sincere conscience bring Christ forth by a holy manner of life which shines as an example to others.'" This motherhood, the nuns explain, is most explicit in the role of their mother abbess, because she "is entrusted in a profoundly specific way with begetting and nourishing Christ in the souls of the sisters. So, she is called 'Mother.'"[7]

---

5   Pope Honorius III, Solet Annuere, *On the Rules of the Friars Minor.* https://www.papalencyclicals.net/hon03/regula-e.htm.
6   Mt 12:50.
7   Community documents and self-printed pamphlets provided by the Roswell Poor Clares.

There are two particular mothers, other than Our Lady of Guadalupe, whom the Roswell Poor Clares especially revere. The first is the saintly foundress of the Poor Clares, Saint Clare herself, and the second is Mother Mary Francis, one of the foundresses of the Roswell community. Mother Mary Francis (1921–2006) was a talented poet, witty writer, and charitable defender of the ancient and living customs of the Poor Clares. Her first book on monastic life, *A Right to be Merry,* was the bestseller of 1956 and utterly smashes any idea that a cloistered nun is out-of-touch, dour, oppressed, or inhuman. Another of her books, *Strange Gods Before Me,* is a marvelous (and funny) take-down of many modern mental vices that can plague religious and laity alike. Mother Mary Francis's windows into cloistered life reveal women who are so wonderfully relatable because they are real women. Mother Mary Francis assured us that, "what is the perfection of womanhood in a married woman or a single woman in the world will be the perfection of womanhood in a sister in a convent or a nun in a monastery."[8]

Mother Mary Francis was entrusted with the important task of writing the updated 1981 Constitutions of the Poor Clare nuns of the Federation of Mary Immaculate in the United States, as was required by the Vatican after the Second Vatican Council. In an era of upheaval, when

---

[8] Mother Mary Francis, P.C.C., "All the Days of Her Life." Self-published pamphlet by the Poor Clare Monastery of Our Lady of Guadalupe.

many orders worried that their age-old customs, habits, and charisms were archaic and not suited for the modern world, Mother Mary Francis wisely saw through the chaos and confusion. She knew that the modern world cried out for a sign of contradiction, a visible mark of religion, and the steady presence of physical symbols that underscored fundamental realities. She wrote lovingly of the cloister, the grille, the habit, the veil. Her Poor Clares sing the praises of their traditional Franciscan way of life: "Are customs stifling? Not if we understand them. And understanding them, we love them. We cherish them. We want to hand them down, perhaps sometimes altered, in essential meaning the same."[9]

As for holy Mother Saint Clare, well, Mother Mary Francis described her spiritual mother best:

> Saint Clare was a woman who seemed born for nothing else but to be cherished by others. No eighteen-year-old ever had a more dazzling future spread out before her. But Clare was not satisfied. Her woman's breast held a poet's heart of such capacity that nothing so small as a world could hope to fill it. Fashioned for loving and nothing else, to be one man's wife was not her fulfillment. So she became the bride of God Himself. To mother

---

[9]   Community documents and self-printed pamphlets provided by the Roswell Poor Clares.

one family of children was not enough. So Clare hid herself in a cloister to mother all the world.[10]

The Benedictines of Mary, Queen of Apostles in Gower, Missouri

Dedicated to the Queen of the Apostles, Mother Cecilia and her fifty-three Benedictine sisters look to Our Lady's hidden life in Ephesus as their model for life. "We take Our Lady's hidden life at Ephesus as an inspiration for our own. We seek to be what she was for the early Church: a loving and prayerful support to the Apostles, the first priests, and daily offer prayer and sacrifice for the sake of her spiritual sons."[11]

If anyone knows anything about Benedictines, it is their motto: *ora et labora,* "pray and work." The greatest treasure in the nuns' daily prayer life is the traditional Latin liturgy. Additionally, following the original Benedictine rule, the nuns chant all one hundred and fifty hymns each week and pray the Latin Divine Office together eight times a day. In choosing Latin, the official language of the Church, the nuns seek to continue in the footsteps of fifteen hundred years of Benedictine prayer.

---

[10]   Mother Mary Francis, P.C.C., "The Poor Clare Life." Excerpted from *A Right to be Merry.* Reprinted via Blurb, Incorporated, 2021 by the Poor Clare Monastery of Our Lady of Guadalupe.
[11]   "Obedience." Benedictines of Mary Queen of Apostles. https ://benedictinesofmary.org/monasticvocation/.

When the nuns work, they not only busy themselves with the daily needs of their monastery, which includes housework and farm chores, but they also produce and sell art to benefit the Church and support the abbey. Drawing from their practice of sung prayer, the nuns make sacred sheet music for church choirs, as well as recorded performances of their monastic chant and hymns. Additionally, following in the tradition of many a monastic artist, they paint and produce original artwork for religiously themed greeting cards and, most impressively of all, craft exquisite handmade vestments for priests. In all their work, the nuns are deeply committed to restoring beauty and giving God the glory. Finally, the nuns carry out the famous Benedictine commitment to hospitality. Also, in keeping with their charism, they operate retreat quarters, which are intended primarily for priests.

As abbess, Mother Cecilia shepherds her community in living out their distinctive Benedictine vows: obedience, conversion of life, and stability. By obedience, the nuns attempt a generous and humble death to self for the sake of following the desires of God. Conversion of life, as described by Pope Gregory the Great, means a radical surrendering of the self as a gift to God: "to leave the world and to give up exterior possessions is perhaps something still easy; but for a man to give up himself, to immolate what is most precious to him by surrendering his entire liberty is much more arduous work: to forsake what one has is a small thing, to forsake what one is, that is the supreme gift."[12] This vow calls the Benedictine to fully surrender to vocation, holding nothing back.

Finally, the Benedictine vow of stability is, as the Benedictines of Mary put it, a recognition that "home is where the heart is." As part of their way of life, Benedictines practice constitutional enclosure, which means that nuns may only leave the cloister for important business concerning the abbey. Contained within this vow is the call to create and foster a family within the confines of the monastery. Benedictines vow to live out their days within a particular monastery, rather than transfer from one to another as one would a job. As the Benedictines of Mary describe this life, "A child is brought up in the home where she will live. So too, the novice is brought up within the family she has chosen, or more properly, the family which God has lovingly chosen for her, from all eternity. The Benedictine of Mary remains and perseveres with her new family. She seeks no other."[13] The nuns visually signify this life-long commitment to their monastery by wearing beautiful lace wedding dresses and veils to make their vows.

As Benedictines, Mother Cecilia and her sisters follow in the footsteps of Saint Benedict and his twin sister, Saint Scholastica. Saint Scholastica, who could be called the mother of western monasticism, was described by Saint Gregory the Great as, "she who could do more because

12 "Obedience." https://benedictinesofmary.org/monasticvocation/.
13 "Obedience." https://benedictinesofmary.org/monasticvocation/.

she loved more."[14] In his account of the life of Saint Benedict, Pope Gregory told this story to demonstrate just how
much Scholastica could accomplish with her love. She
and her brother, Benedict, only visited each other once
a year. To do so, they would leave their monasteries and
meet in the middle at a little farmhouse. Once, as Benedict was getting ready to leave, Scholastica begged her
brother to stay longer, but he refused. Scholastica put her
hands together in prayer and immediately, a great light-
ning storm arose. Shocked, Benedict asked, "What have
you done, sister?" And she replied, "Since my brother
refused, I asked my God."[15] The siblings visited together
for the rest of the night. Only a few days later, Scholastica
passed away. God rewarded her great love, and women
from across the world have flocked to become her spiritual daughters for over fifteen hundred years.

The Benedictines of Mary, Queen of Apostles, are
blessed with another holy mother looking over their
monastic family. In 2023, the nuns discovered that the
body of their community's foundress, Mother Wilhelmina (1924–2019) was inexplicably incorrupt. Sister Wilhelmina was born Mary Elizabeth Lancaster in
Saint Louis, Missouri. The descendant of black slaves, the
future Benedictine grew up in the landscape of Jim Crow.
Her parents founded a Catholic school for black children

---

[14]   Pope Gregory the Great, *The Dialogues of St. Gregory the Great.*
Edmund G. Gardner, editor. Philip Lee Warner Press, (London:
1911), 95.
[15]   Pope Gregory the Great, *The Dialogues of St. Gregory the Great,* 95.

that was eventually folded into the diocesan school system during desegregation.

Sister Wilhelmina joined the Oblate Sisters of Providence—a historically black order in the United States—immediately after high school. Unfortunately, her order, like so many in the second half of the twentieth century, abandoned their traditional way of monastic life. For years, Sister Wilhelmina was the lone sister in a habit—which she made herself. Finally, in 1995, as an elderly woman, she founded the community that would quickly become the Benedictines of Mary, Queen of Apostles, aided by the Priestly Fraternity of Saint Peter.[16]

A faithful adherent to the ancient traditions of the Church, Mother Wilhelmina and her witness to Christian unity and charity is a treasure in the crown of American Catholicism. While the Church has, as of the writing of this book, not yet made an official pronouncement on what appears to be her miraculous incorruptibility, several people who have visited her body at the monastery have begun to testify to miracles worked through her intercession. God willing, in a few years, the Benedictines can witness the canonization of their own spiritual mother.

[16] Kelsey Wicks, "Who was Sister Wilhelmina Lancaster, whose body is now the center of attention in Missouri?" Catholic News Agency, May 24, 2023. https://www.catholicnewsagency.com/news/254413/who-was-sister-wilhelmina-lancaster-the-african-american-whose-body-is-potentially-incorrupt.

Holy Annunciation Monastery of the Byzantine Discalced Carmelites in Sugarloaf, Pennsylvania

Nestled into Pennsylvania's Pocono Mountains is a monastery where the two lungs of the Church, East and West, breathe as one. Holy Annunciation Monastery of the Byzantine Discalced Carmelites is led by its Foundress, Hegumena (abbess) Mother Marija. In the 1970s, Mother Marija and two fellow Roman-rite Discalced Carmelites answered the invitation of Byzantine bishop Michael Dudick to bring the Carmelite tradition to his eparchy (diocese) and become the first ever Eastern-rite Carmel. The monastery has been blessed with growth over the years, attracting entrants from around the world.

As Carmelites, the sisters practice solitude within the structure of community, adhering to Saint Teresa of Ávila's admonition that nuns should pray without ceasing. As Eastern Christians in communion with Rome, they worship using the Divine Liturgy of Saint John Chrysostom as well as live by Eastern monastic practices, such as their traditional eastern monastic garb and monastic structures. Thus, while they are a branch of the great tradition of the Carmelites, they follow their own Typicon (constitutions) in the tradition of Eastern monasticism, which is not organized into specific religious orders. Rather, each monastery is its own "order," and any daughter community would function under a different Typicon. The monastery is also still part of the Carmelite Federation, however.

Their chapel, graced with its distinctive golden onion domes, was largely built by their own hands when the funding fell through for contractors to finish its interior. The walls and ceiling were lovingly covered with magnificent iconography by the hand of an Orthodox iconographer, Constantine Youssis. Constantine is also renowned among both Byzantines and Orthodox faithful as the painter of a miraculous weeping icon of the *Theotokos,* housed in Chicago.

To harmonize their eastern and western influences, the monastery also follows the rule of Saint Benedict of Nursia. Saint Benedict was a pre-schism era saint, cherished both by the east and west as the Father of Western Monasticism, who was deeply inspired by the Eastern Desert Fathers. The Byzantine Carmelites also draw inspiration from the Trappistine order in their mission to be "the link with the Great Undivided Church, when monastics were friends—brothers and sisters to each other."[17] The sisters' charism highlights unity between East and West, and they pray especially for the end of divisions in the Church and between Christians.

Following the ancient practice of monastics supporting themselves by their own hands, the sisters carry out

---

[17]   "Our History." Holy Annunciation Monastery. Ruthenian Catholic Nuns. https://www.byzantinediscalcedcarmelites.com/page3.html.

a robust tradition of manual labor. They produce baked goods, yogurt, and preserves to sell through their Monastery Pantry, selling items both locally and online—and as my children will attest, their apricot rolls are a foretaste of Heaven! They are especially busy at Christmas and Easter, specializing in Eastern European pastries and festal breads. Additionally, facilitated by the fact that their monastery is built on a former farm, the nuns also run the Carmelite Mini Corral, where they breed and sell internationally acclaimed miniature show horses and miniature jersey milk cows, boasting a truly jaw-dropping trophy collection.

Mother Marija told me that her path to becoming a foundress of such a unique monastery was a series of "divine landmines." God allowed explosions to occur throughout her more than seventy years as a professed religious. These explosions redirected her steps from her charted course until she found herself answering this call that was as deeply dear to her heart as it was entirely unexpected. In the uproar of the 60s, she was bounced from one shuttering Carmel to another, trying to live her vocation faithfully in a world where fewer and fewer of her fellow religious seemed to care anymore. From this chaos of disunity, her vision for Holy Annunciation Monastery was one of divine unity and harmony. The establishment of the monastery has been a project of deep faith and trust in God and His watchful care.

Valley of Our Lady Monastery of the Cistercian Nuns in Prairie du Sac, Wisconsin

Sister Anne Marie is the superior of the Cistercian Nuns of the Valley of Our Lady Monastery in Prairie du Sac, Wisconsin, in the Diocese of Madison; the only monastery of Cistercian nuns of the Ancient Observance in the United States. The monastery was founded in 1957 by Swiss Cistercian nuns from the 11th century Abbey of Frauenthal, which also means "Valley of Our Lady" in German.[18]

Cistercians are an ancient off-shoot of the Benedictine Order: in the eleventh century, French Benedictines at the Abbey of Citeaux decided that they wanted to follow the rule of Saint Benedict even more closely to the original and organized their life around the *Carta Caritatis*, or "Charter of Charity," which emphasizes manual labor and a life of prayer and austerity. One of the great Doctors of the Church, St. Bernard of Clairvaux—also called the "Honeyed Doctor" and the "Marian Doctor" because of his beautiful writings—joined the newly formed Cistercians and was a huge influence upon the order.

Saint Bernard of Clairvaux instilled a deep devotion to Our Lady as mother into his order, which added nuns to

---

[18] "Cistercian Nuns Our History." https://www.valleyofourlady .org/frauenthal.html.

their rapidly expanding numbers in the year 1125. One of Saint Bernard's nicknames is "Mary's Troubadour," due to his beautiful poetry and hymns in honor of the Mother of God. He particularly loved calling Our Lady the "Star of the Sea" and giving homilies on the topic of the Annunciation and Nativity. Once, according to tradition, Saint Bernard was kneeling in prayer before a statue of the Madonna and Child. This was a special sort of statue—one that was fairly common in the Middle Ages, but which has sadly been neglected in modern times. It is called a "Nursing Madonna" because Our Lady is depicted nursing Baby Jesus. Kneeling before this image, St. Bernard exclaimed, "Show yourself a mother!" The image immediately projected milk at him! According to some versions of the story, the milk sprinkled upon his lips; in others, it went into his eye. In all versions of the story, Our Lady's miraculous milk gave St. Bernard spiritual clarity and wisdom to sing the praises of the Mother of God.[19]

At the Valley of Our Lady Monastery in Wisconsin, the twenty-three sisters walk in the footsteps of St. Bernard and a thousand years of Cistercian monks and nuns. Part of the reform that led to the creation of the Cistercian order was a re-emphasis upon manual labor to support the monastery. As the nuns carry out their daily work, they remind themselves that "every work is

---

[19]   James France, "The Heritage of Saint Bernard in Medieval Art." *A Companion to Bernard of Clairvaux*. Brian Patrick McGuire, editor. (Brill: 2011), 330.

equally valuable if done in the spirit of service, obedience, and the love of Christ."[20] Labor is, of course, married to prayer. The nuns' day has nine discrete times set apart for prayer, not counting daily Mass. The nuns pray the Liturgy of the Hours in Latin with Gregorian chant.

In the initial years of the monastery, the nuns were also dairy farmers, since their monastery occupies the historic farmstead once owned by a former governor of Wisconsin. Alas, in the 1960s, a fire destroyed the dairy barn, then the largest in the state. Since the loss of their dairy, the monastery shifted to support themselves by baking hundreds of communion wafers intended for consecration at Masses across twenty-seven states.

The nuns carefully attend to the historic buildings of their monastic farmstead but have found that they cannot keep ahead of the maintenance needed for those nineteenth century walls. Additionally, while the contemplative Cistercian charism is to seek stillness and solitude, modern developments are beginning to surround the monastery. Thus, the nuns are engaged in a bold effort to construct a new monastery, built to purpose on a different, extremely rural property that will allow them space for the many vocations with which they continue to be blessed.

The new monastery, the nuns say, is intended to "be a witness to every dimension of our Roman Catholic faith: witnessing to Truth, Goodness, and Beauty; and to be the

---

[20] "Cistercian Nuns Work." https://www.valleyofourlady.org/cistercianwork.html.

spiritual and moral necessity of building in a responsible and theological way through traditional forms of architecture."[21] The nuns' aim is to build according to the style of early Cistercian architecture, with low reliance upon modern technology. Sketches of the proposed chapel, especially, are breathtaking, harnessing the traditional Cistercian love of raw stone and natural light in a liturgical style in which St. Bernard of Clairvaux himself would feel at home.

As their foundress, Mother Magdalen said, "The way is long, the way is far, but God is with us, so we are not afraid."[22]

The Capuchin Sisters of Nazareth, Mother of God Convent in Tunkhannock, Pennsylvania, St. Joseph's Convent, Jackson, PA, and Mother of the Eucharist Convent, Bastress, PA

Sisters Colette, Clare, Christina, and Joseph are all members of the Capuchin Sisters of Nazareth. According to their monastic constitutions, "The Eucharist is the beating heart of the convent where the brides are in union with their bridegroom and their prayers continually burn on the altar of their hearts. Here, the bride is made one

---

[21]   "Purpose." For the Glory of God, Valley of Our Lady Monastery. https://build.valleyofourlady.org/the-project/.
[22]   "Purpose." https://build.valleyofourlady.org/the-project/.

with her spouse."[23] At each of the Capuchin Sisters' three convents in eastern Pennsylvania, these brides of Christ strive to embody the hidden, domestic life of the Holy Family at Nazareth. As their constitutions further state, "it was in Nazareth that Jesus lived his hidden life, where Our Lady received her call, and it was the place that Jesus was identified with on the Cross."[24]

The Capuchin Sisters of Nazareth are both a new order and a very old one. As a new order, they trace their founding to 1995, when two biological sisters began a community, originally based in Massachusetts. As an old order, the sisters trace their religious lineage from the sixteenth century Capuchin reforms to the Franciscan order from the thirteenth century. These early Capuchin reformers sought a life that radically followed that of Saint Francis himself, re-emphasizing his original poverty and humility in ways that the main branch of the Franciscan order had adjusted in the intervening centuries.

As such, the Capuchin Sisters of Nazareth hold, as Saint Francis himself said, that poverty is "the mother and queen of all virtues."[25] This means that the sisters limit their worldly possessions as much as possible and rely almost exclusively upon the charity of others,

---

[23]   "Prayer." https://www.capuchinfranciscansisters.com/franciscan-charism.

[24]   "Capuchin Sisters of Nazareth." https://www.capuchinfranciscan sisters.com/.

[25]   Community informational documents.

even to the point of occasionally begging for alms. In exchange for the generosity of others, the sisters, like thousands of Capuchins and Franciscans before them, offer prayers of thanksgiving, "the gift that supersedes all others."[26]

Unlike their fellow daughters of Saint Francis, the Poor Clares, the Capuchin sisters are contemplative but not cloistered. They describe themselves as "apostolic contemplatives," which means that they foster a hidden, contemplative charism akin to the quiet life of Christ in Nazareth before his public ministry. The apostolic nature of their contemplative life asks the sisters to be more engaged with the world about them than is practiced by some other contemplative charisms.

As part of their Franciscan tradition of preaching, the sisters conduct parish missions and youth retreats. However, their major focus, as contemplatives, is to pray. In addition to the Liturgy of the Hours, for these Capuchins, prayer takes the form of Eucharistic adoration: the sisters attend daily Mass and two periods of Eucharistic adoration each day, once right after rising in the morning, the other right before dinner in the evening. Religious life lived faithfully, joyfully, and lovingly is their chief form of preaching: a quiet testimony to a world that is in desperate need of radical witness.

The Capuchin sisters also cherish their communal life in the convent. They cultivate the family of the convent,

---

[26]   Community informational documents.

"a true family where their joy, as Brides of Christ, witnesses to the world the good news of the Gospel."[27] They emphasize that it is this communal, family life that allows them to remain faithful to their religious vows and charism: "the sisters would unanimously agree that without this common life, the sacrifices and disciplines of Religious Life would be extremely difficult. It is much easier, for example, to rise for the night vigil, to fast, to observe periods of silence, knowing that the community is doing the same."[28] This communal life is an extremely important element of their Franciscan identity.

In addition to their life of prayer, contemplation, and radical poverty, the Capuchin Sisters of Nazareth raise cats and German shepherd dogs. They wear the humble yet beautiful Capuchin robes—their warm, earthy color is responsible for the name of cappuccino coffee, and where Capuchin monkeys get their name—although the sisters wear more feminine veils instead of the famous *capuch* hoods of their Capuchin brothers.

---

[27] Community informational documents.
[28] Community informational documents.

CHAPTER 2

The Calling of Motherhood

"And Mary said, 'Behold, I am the handmaid of the
Lord; let it be to me according to your word.'"

—Lk 1:38

O ur Lady's *fiat*, her humble embrace of the calling
which God asked of her, are the most important
words ever spoken by a woman. Just imagine: a young
girl called upon to become the mother of God Himself,
to bear the Messiah about whom prophets had spoken
since the very first woman, Eve, had said no to the divine
plan. Mary, however, was so open to the will of God that
when she was asked, she answered immediately, holding
nothing back. Mary's *fiat* made her both the mother of
God and the mother of the entire human race.

There is so much fear these days of saying yes, a fear
that has reached crisis levels in the Church. We can
debate the various causes for it, but starting in the 20th
century, more and more Christians have been saying
"no," "not yet," and "never!" far more than we have been

saying, "let it be done to me according to your word." Statistics suggest that only 50% of American Catholics are married and of them, fewer than 70% have a sacramental marriage.[29] As for religious life, well, that is even more depressing—since 1970, those answering the call to religious life has dropped by over 75%.[30] People are terrified of commitment or have been convinced by the world that commitment isn't necessary for a happy, fulfilling life—in fact, that commitment might get in the way of it!

The world wants us to be free, unattached, and ready for any new adventure. A vocation with its demanding vows just imposes so many obstacles. Making a life-long commitment to one thing—one spouse, one family, one monastery, one charism—just does not make much sense in the fast-moving world of today. Even many Catholics have fallen into this mindset—shouldn't we treat life like the ancient Hebrews at the first Passover, with our shoes on and our staff in our hand, ready for whatever mission God might call us tomorrow? Lots of well-meaning Catholics worry that saying yes to a traditional vocation might tie them up and make them less useful to God.

---

[29] Pew Research Center, "U.S. CATHOLICS OPEN TO NON-TRADITIONAL FAMILIES." September 2, 2015. https://www.pew research.org/religion/2015/09/02/u-s-catholics-open-to-non -traditional-families/.
[30] Michael Lipka, "U.S. nuns face shrinking numbers and tensions with the Vatican," Pew Research Center. August 8, 2014. https://www .pewresearch.org/short-reads/2014/08/08/u-s-nuns-face-shrinking -numbers-and-tensions-with-the-vatican/.

But the thrilling secret of vocations is that the world has it all backward. It is through those solemn, sacred vows made before God that we really become useful for the Church and the world. It is only through the constraints of obedience, faithfulness, and stability that we stand a chance to break past our personal limitations and become free. Saying yes to our calling and binding ourselves to it through the solemn and sacred rites which the Church has established over the millennia is the most exciting adventure we could ever imagine.

For us Christian women, whether we are called to marriage and physical motherhood or to religious life and spiritual motherhood, saying yes to our vocation is not simply an echo of Mary's *fiat*, but also a commitment to become like her for our families and communities. Far from being presumptuous to think of ourselves like the Queen of Heaven, it is exactly what God expects of us. Saint Paul, in his letter to the Ephesians, compares husbands to Christ: "For the husband is the head of the wife as Christ is the head of the church, his body, and is himself its Savior."[31] Husbands and fathers—both lay and religious—take Christ the King as their role model. As Christians, we are all called to become Christ-like. But as men, fathers are called to model Christ in a very particular, masculine way. Similarly, women have been given the glorious mother of all creation as our own feminine model and goal. As Pope Saint John Paul II reminds

---

[31]   Eph 5:22–23.

us, "In [Mary] the vocation to motherhood reached the summit of its dignity and potential."[32]

Question

Both of the ancient vocations which the Church has offered women are focused around the idea of motherhood. In the married vocation, wives promise to accept children from God and fulfill the role of motherhood, while in the religious vocation, nuns are described as spiritual mothers. What is a spiritual mother and what does it share with a physical mother?

Answer by Sister Clare, Capuchin Sisters of Nazareth

Saint Francis of Assisi would say to his Friars:

"If a mother nourishes and loves her own son (cf. 1 Th 2:7) according to the flesh, how much more diligently ought he love and nourish his own spiritual brother?"[33]

The same can be said for our sisters in religious life, the people we live with day to day. How do we "nourish and cherish" them? We cook for each other, we clean up after each other, we serve, love, and respect one another; but

[32]   John Paul II, "Angelus." Valle d'Aosta, Sunday July 16, 1995. https://www.vatican.va/content/john-paul-ii/it/angelus/1995/documents/hf_jp-ii_ang_19950716.html.
[33]   Francis of Assisi, *The Writings of St. Francis of Assisi.* Translated from the Critical Latin Edition of Fr. Kajetan Esser, O.F.M. A Publication of the Franciscan Archive. 1999. 79. http://www.catholicapologetics.info/library/onlinelibrary/Opus.pdf.

just as a mother doesn't do these things for her children out of "duty," so we sisters strive to do these things out of *love* for Christ, who is present within each sister. A mother doesn't see herself as a servant or slave unless there is no love, and she is resentful of her life. When a woman is a mother who loves, even the most menial tasks (like changing diapers or running errands) are not below her dignity because it is *her place* in the family. We can see these tasks as opportunities to love or as degrading duties that must get done in the drudgery of the day; this is what makes a world of difference.

A spiritual mother (a consecrated religious, for example) is not *only* a mother for her sisters. Pope Saint John Paul II wrote in his Encyclical, "The Dignity of Woman":

> Virginity according to the Gospel means renouncing marriage and thus physical motherhood. Nevertheless, the renunciation of this kind of motherhood, a renunciation that can involve great sacrifice for a woman, makes possible a different kind of motherhood: a motherhood 'according to the Spirit' (Romans 8:4). For virginity does not deprive a woman of her prerogatives. Spiritual motherhood takes on many forms . . . and it can express itself as a concern for each and every person . . . a special readiness to be poured out for (them).[34]

---

[34]   John Paul II, *Mulieris Dignitatem*, 1988. https://www.vatican .va/content/john-paul-ii/en/apost_letters/1988/documents/hf_jp-ii _apl_19880815_mulieris-dignitatem.html.

Doesn't a physical mother often find herself "poured out" taking care of the needs of her children? She patiently teaches, encourages, helps, corrects, comforts, and all without realizing that, in this patient care, lies true humility and greatness. For a woman's heart is made to be "a shelter in which other souls may unfold"[35] (St. Edith Stein), and her motherhood only finds fulfillment when she is carrying these other souls.

As a spiritual mother, a religious pours herself out in sacrifice, the sacrifice of her very person, and so her motherhood is no less fruitful and thus very fulfilling. Her child is *every soul!* She encourages, teaches, leads them to the truth, prays for their conversion, their strength, their well-being, and ultimately gives birth and life to them at the foot of the cross, where she entrusts them to their Redeemer (her spouse) day and night. Fulfilling? Definitely! Rewarding? Not often . . . but it will be in heaven, no doubt!

How many mothers grieve over a child who has left the faith or simply rebels against everything they were raised to believe, and this without any explanation? The silence and solitary suffering of a mother's heart in these moments can only be compared to the silence and solitude of a religious adoring her God in faith, before the tabernacle for all His straying children.

---

[35]   Edith Stein, *Fundamental Principles of Women's Education.* https://www.kolbefoundation.org/gbookswebsite/studentlibrary /greatestbooks/aaabooks/stein/principleswomeneducation.html.

Sacrificial love is at the heart of spiritual mother-hood, as it is in physical motherhood. The hidden sac-rifices and deep sufferings a mother endures for her family are the most powerful examples of true and self-less love! For a religious, these look like: breaking our sleep at 2 a.m. every night to meet our Spouse in the chapel, surrendering our time and our wills in obedi-ence, spending hours of silent prayer before the taber-nacle, the silent endurance of interior struggles in the spiritual life—often offered for someone going through a similar experience—and of course, the hundreds of heart-rending prayer requests from people suffering intensely, people who need a motherly word of com-fort and a prayer of intercession placed before the Lord. Ours is the role of the Mother-of-all-mothers, Mary, who *stood* and watched her son suffer in agony. No one could recount what her heart bore for love of Him and His children!

All mothers (physical or spiritual) are, in all hon-esty, truly *helpless*. We care passionately for others, yet are often rewarded with indifference, ingratitude, and outright rebellion. Yet our strength lies, as Mary's did, in the offering, in *giving*. And how could God refuse to hear the prayers and pleas of one who resembles His own Sorrowful Mother?

Question

I was talking with a new mom friend of mine, and she admitted to me that, two months into being a mom, she felt like she had lost her identity. She loved her baby, obviously, but didn't feel like she was the person she had always been before. When we embrace the vocation of motherhood, we must give up so much of who and what we were. We aren't really "ourselves" anymore, and never will be again, because motherhood has made us forever different—I will always be a mother now. There is no "going back" and no "taking a break." A lot of new moms find that scary. Taking permanent vows as a nun is also a drastic altering of yourself, and you too must forever surrender that person you had been outside of the cloister. How do we manage that part of our vocations—the call to surrender ourselves in this way?

Answer by Mother Marija, Byzantine Carmelites

Happiness, I think, really comes from peace. Yes, that's the whole thing. Babies are happy with themselves, because there is no reason to be unhappy! Nobody told them to be unhappy. That is an important thing. God, in creating the world, wanted not simply to create something He could enjoy. No, He was really creating an entire creation which would be infused with divinity. And through Original Sin, as far as we are concerned, we lost our inclusion in that divinity.

The divinity of the Incarnation: Christ's mission was not just to satisfy His Father. He was not simply paying the penalty for something that we had done wrong. No. It was not just that sort of situation. God wanted humanity to be infused with divinity, gathering the whole of humanity into the Trinity. This is what the Eastern Church calls *Theosis*. We do not become a deity, but we have the deity. The deity—God—has transformed us. That's a big difference.

I was reading something in Saint Gregory the other day, that after the Fall, God saw humanity lying dead. It was all over for us. So, in response, the grand intention of God in the Incarnation was that He would become as humanity was, so that humanity would be drawn up into His divinity and live again. That is an incredible thought. He stooped over this dead thing and pulled it up to where He had first wanted it to be: in Himself. Every part of our humanity, in Christ, is divinity. And then, in order to "get back" to His Father, Christ has to bring all the rest of humanity with Him—there is no going alone! If you look at an icon of the Harrowing of Hell, you see Christ's hands are full of strength. Adam and Eve's hands are just limp, and He is holding them with his strong ones. It says so much of what this mystery is about.

So, to get back to your question: the body in each of us has to be tamed. Whatever your struggle might be, that is not what is actually important. What is important is that faith in the redemption of humanity that will bring us back to divinity. That is what we are trying to do in our vocations; that when we die, we not only find that our debt has been paid, but that we now participate in the original plan of creation—not to simply be an object of pleasure for the Creator, but to share in His divinity.

Question

I know so many women who suffer from infertility. These are married women who would make the best mothers who either have not been granted any children, or who have suffered countless miscarriages, or who have a few children but feel called to have a large family and yet cannot. There are also a lot of monasteries out there— faithful ones—which are also suffering from an infertility of vocations. There is a rather hurtful attitude among some Catholics that not being blessed with an abundance, either of children or of vocations, is a sign that you are doing it wrong. What would you say to those who are being faithful to God's vision for their vocation and yet suffer this terrible burden?

Answer by Mother Mary Angela and the Roswell Poor Clares

The first response from the community was simply, "Don't give up!" God has His own time, and we must wait on Him and for that time to come.

Many married couples experience infertility, adopt a child, and then have the joy of bearing children of their own. We also remembered Holy Mother Colette, who was born "late" in the normal human course of things. Although this seems to have been of a miraculous nature, it reminds us that the Lord can do whatever He wants, whenever He wants! But if God does not bless the marriage with children, we remember that children are not the only "point" of marriage, that the nurturing of one another as husband and wife is also very important.

There are many other ways to serve God and nurture life when natural parenthood is not a possibility: taking up charitable apostolates such as hosting Bible studies or other youth groups in one's own home, being a parental figure in the lives of young people in need, helping other families with children. We know of one woman who was not able to have children of her own, but her siblings ask her to help with their children, and this is an all-around blessing.

The longing of childless couples for children must be very pleasing to God, and surely makes some reparation for those who have chosen abortion for their children, as well as for those who prefer not to have children for selfish reasons.

In a monastic community, it can be a time of deep growth for the community when there are no novitiate sisters—we can grow in the understanding of our own vocation at such a time and in the appreciation of the greatness of the gift of new vocations to our community. We have experienced times of "vocational drought" and know that it is very painful, but such times also call us to examine how faithfully and fully we are living out our own vocation.

Success in God's eyes is not always success in human eyes. We think of one community that has not been blessed with persevering vocations for many years, but the sisters continue to live our Poor Clare life with deep faith, hope, and trusting love. That community may be far more "successful" in God's eyes than one that is abounding in vocations, and a small community may be much more pleasing in God's eyes than a large one! Only the Lord knows. Meanwhile, each community is called to live their vocation to the best of their ability and trust in His goodness. In the end, this is what really matters.

Whether we are speaking of married couples or religious communities, we want to revisit the need for "healthy boundaries." Even if others think that a lack of children or a lack of vocations is a sign we are doing something wrong, and even if this is something painful, it is not really the most important thing. The most important thing is the steady desire of our hearts to please God and to accept His will, whatever it may be—and to trust that His will is the best thing for us.

The Magnificat—Our Lady's Prayer of Thanksgiving[36]

My soul magnifies the Lord,

and my spirit rejoices in God my Savior,

for he has regarded the low estate
of his handmaiden.

For behold, henceforth all generations will
call me blessed;

for he who is mighty has done great things for me,

and holy is his name.

And his mercy is on those who fear him

from generation to generation.

He has shown strength with his arm,

he has scattered the proud in the
imagination of their hearts,

he has put down the mighty from their thrones,

and exalted those of low degree;

he has filled the hungry with good things,

and the rich he has sent empty away.

He has helped his servant Israel,

in remembrance of his mercy,

as he spoke to our fathers,

to Abraham and to his posterity for ever.

---

[36] Lk 1:46–55.

CHAPTER 3

Motherhood and True Femininity

"The woman's soul is fashioned as a shelter
in which other souls may unfold."

—Saint Teresa Benedicta of the Cross (Edith Stein)

The fact that women's vocations are centered around motherhood underscores something magnificent about our distinct feminine nature. Whether God calls us to physical motherhood or spiritual motherhood, He has crafted vocations for us that harmonize with our femininity and allow us to develop that which is essential in us as women specifically. Whether we are blessed to hold children inside us or, as Saint Teresa Benedicta of the Cross said, called to shelter their souls for a time, all women are designed as vessels for the nourishment and development of human life.

Of course, women can be called to do many other things in addition to this primary calling, as we have been gifted by God with such a variety of talents and desires. However, the modern world would have us believe that motherhood is just one option among a broad swath of career or lifestyle choices. But this is not true. At various points in our lives as women, we might be called to use our talents as teachers, scientists, writers, entrepreneurs, and more.

But whatever else we are asked to do with our lives, we are all called to some form of motherhood. Alice von Hildebrand tells us that, a "woman by her very nature is maternal—for every woman, whether married or unmarried, is called upon to be a biological, psychological, or spiritual mother—she knows intuitively that to give, to nurture, to care for others, to suffer with and for them—for maternity implies suffering—is infinitely more valuable in God's sight than to conquer nations and fly to the moon."[37]

It is for this reason that, traditionally, the popes have spoken out against social changes that have forced many women out of the home to find supplementary income. Pope Pius XI, for instance, in *Quadragesimo Anno*, insisted that, "Mothers, concentrating on household duties, should work primarily in the home or in its immediate vicinity. It is an intolerable abuse, and to be abolished at all cost, for mothers on account of the father's low wage to be forced to engage in gainful occupations

---

[37]   Alice von Hildebrand, "Alice Von Hildebrandt on Feminism and Femininity," NEW ROCHELLE, New York, 26 Nov. 2003 (ZENIT).

outside the home to the neglect of their proper cares and duties, especially the training of children."[38]

Of course, such a stance immediately raises hackles, even in fairly conservative circles. This emphasis upon a mother's role is deeply unpopular, and the Church has been attacked for having a "backwards" stance about gender and feminism. There is a widespread attitude that the world needs what women have to offer, but what mainstream society means by that is a rather confused jumble. What is it exactly about women specifically that is needed? To secular eyes, an emphasis upon motherhood as the essential feminine quality is embarrassing, even demeaning. The world would rather define women as fierce, defiant, independent . . . all things that are not essential to our feminine nature.

The world shies away from the reality that we are called to nurture, love, suffer, and humbly participate in the divine act of creation itself. When the modern world hears Pius XI's term, "household duties," it typically imagines women relegated to cleaning, cooking, and other chores. But that is only a surface level understanding of what it means to nurture a home. Naturally, somebody has to clean a house, lest it become an uninviting den, unfit for love to flourish. Similarly, someone has to cook, lest the household wither from neglect.

---

[38]   Pius XI, *Quadragesimo Anno.* https://www.vatican.va/content /pius-xi/en/encyclicals/documents/hf_p-xi_enc_19310515_quad ragesimo-anno.html.

However, to assume that these sorts of things are what a mother *does* is to mistake a part for the whole. In another letter, *Casti Connubi*, Pius XI describes the mother as sitting upon a "truly regal throne" in the center of her home.[39] When the world reacts in anger to the thought that a woman's primary calling is to tend the domestic hearth, it cannot see our real household duties. And what an amazing calling it is: to usher souls into this world as a divinely ordained sub-creator, to nurture them when they are young, and to give them wings to fly toward God Himself.

Question

The progressive attitude awash in society wants us to think of parents as gender neutral. So many people assume that "father" and "mother" are interchangeable terms for someone who is the caretaker of their children. But as Christians, we know that fatherhood and motherhood are both more sacred and unique than that. After all, we are taught that God is our heavenly Father, not simply a divine parent. We also know that He wanted us to have a mother, and so He gave us the Virgin Mary, who is so much more than just the physical means by which Christ came into the world. Being a religious mother, you are also called to be more than an administrator of a collection of women. What have you discovered about this distinctive role of a mother?

---

[39]   Pius XI, *Casti Connubi*. https://www.vatican.va/content/pius-xi /en/encyclicals/documents/hf_p-xi_enc_19301231_casti-connubii .html.

Answer by Mother Mary Angela and the Roswell Poor Clares

This is a very large question, and I believe it would take a book to answer it thoroughly! While the gift of serving as the mother abbess of a religious community differs in many ways from the gift of natural motherhood, there are many wonderful similarities. The role of the mother abbess is that of spiritual motherhood, which blends the service of authority with the tenderness of maternity.

All authority is ordered toward growth, whether in the family or the religious community. It is a great help in religious life if the community understands that authority, rules, and regulations exist to help us grow, not to diminish our freedom. The same can be said for discipline. When the spiritual mother has to correct, she tries to avoid "laying down the law" but seeks to point out the ideal, and she seeks to help a sister understand and seek the freedom that comes from obedience to God's law.

Spiritual maternity is expressed in love that nurtures each individual and seeks to help each sister grow to be the religious woman that God desires her to be. This means growth at all levels: spiritual, intellectual, social, human, and most importantly, as brides of Christ and as spiritual mothers themselves. This means looking for opportunities to help sisters grow, whether as a community or on the individual level, and helping the sisters to identify God's call to growth in the daily events of life.

The mother of a family, be it religious or natural, has a critical role in determining the atmosphere of family life. This means cultivating an atmosphere of warm charity, ready forgiveness, mutual respect, and appreciation in community; first by striving to practice these virtues herself. Her deep and genuine respect for each person has a permeative effect upon the "climate" of community life—her courtesy, thoughtfulness, readiness to sacrifice for the good of her sisters, her sincere interest in all that interests them, etc.

That said, the highest priority for the spiritual mother has to be prayer! Praying for her sisters can often change the whole dynamic of a "problem," and it deepens the understanding of a situation like nothing else can. The Holy Spirit can, in a wonderful way, help the spiritual mother to understand better what a sister is experiencing, how she sees things. It also reminds the spiritual mother that everything does not depend on her, but on God, and that she is simply His instrument. Praying to the sister's guardian angel and to her patron saint is also a very effective way to deepen a spiritual bond with her.

Question

A struggle Christian mothers often deal with is the world's judgment about how we conduct ourselves as mothers. This is especially true for stay-at-home mothers, homeschool mothers, and mothers of large families. We don't conform to the world's idea of a normal, successful person. While I feel that the choices I have made as a mother are ones which Christ has asked me to make, it still hurts at times to feel like an oddball, especially when family and friends do not understand, are not accepting of my choices, and are not gentle in their criticism. As a mother superior, you no doubt have had to counsel members of your community who have struggled with the judgment of the world. How do you handle it?

Answer by Sister Anne Marie, Cistercians of the Valley of Our Lady

You (the mother or the religious sister) are called to live by and with the courage of your convictions. The virtue of fortitude is the virtue being exercised. "Choices . . . which Christ has asked me to make." This is your conviction: Christ has asked this; what He asks is good both for me personally and for my family; I want to obey my Lord and Savior and I want to do it courageously and "with conviction". The world's way will always be at odds with Jesus and His Gospel: "If the world hates you, know that it has hated me before it hated you."[40]

Among your more "worldly" friends and relatives, you seem to them to be an oddball. Among those desiring and striving to follow Jesus more closely, you are not an oddball. You are one who is chosen and given the honor and privilege of being His witness. We step back and ask

---

40   Jn 15:18.

ourselves: What is a little hurt and suffering in the light of such an honor and privilege? We need to be far more concerned when the way we are living our life lines up rather nicely with what the world thinks of as "the good life" and as "success." Since it is Jesus who calls us to live the more radical way He lays out for us in the Gospel, He will provide the needed graces.

Having the needed graces does not necessarily make it *easy*, it makes acceptance of the hurt and suffering possible. What we mostly suffer from is our pulling away or our lack of acceptance. Once we really accept what God calls us to, the most painful part of the hurt and suffering is absorbed in love. As the love deepens, a joy that is from the Holy Spirit begins to *show*. Not that we set about to make a show of it—no! Yet the joy will become evident to those around us, including your more worldly friends and relatives.

This joy from the Holy Spirit is something the worldly people will have a difficult time arguing with. It may even be the means that the Holy Spirit will use to win them over to the more radical way of following Jesus as He lays out for us in His Gospel.

Question

A fear I have as a mother is how to raise my daughters to be authentic women in a world that assaults the very idea of true femininity and tries to make us anything and everything but that. I still have many years to go until my little girls become teenagers and young women, but do you have any advice about how to shepherd young women to embrace the call to become women after Our Lady's heart?

Answer by Mother Abbess Cecilia, Benedictines

Here, G. K. Chesterton is a wonderful advocate against the idea of feminism, which has crashed into families even in traditional circles. So much of the world harps upon the fact that women are somehow missing out on something. By this, they are overlooking the great grace and gift that is naturally ours in womanhood.

Women are naturally intuitive, and to listen to the world that tries to masculinize them is to forsake the interior greatness of which they are capable. On the other hand, if they look to Christ and ask the protection of St. Joseph, they will find the protection of the interior light, the support they need, and the security necessary to persevere. All too often, women settle for second best. All that glitters is not gold. It seems we must keep the gold before our eyes, the gold standard of Our Lord Himself and St. Joseph. This is the company in which Our Lady preserved her own femininity.

Our Lady offers us a beautiful example of fully realizing the power as *Virgo Potens*, yet always being available both in prayer and in service. This is what made Our Lady of Sorrows the Queen of Martyrs as well. She is the valiant woman described in the Book of Wisdom. In enduring all the trials, sorrows, and sufferings of daily life without complaint, she was able to sustain the greater ones of the cross later on. This is the fortitude of womanhood, which far outshines that of men.

Our Lady is also the Cause of Our Joy and always delighted in little things. I think this is also the strength of womanhood, to be happy in the little things God sends. Our Lady was joyful in spite of her suffering, and she wants to see her daughters joyful as well.

Novena Prayer to Saint Ann[41]

O glorious Saint Ann, you are filled with compassion for those who invoke you and with love for those who suffer. Heavily burdened with the weight of my troubles, I cast myself at your feet and humbly beg of you to take the present intention, which I recommend to you in your special care. Please recommend it to your daughter, the Blessed Virgin Mary, and place it before the throne of Jesus, so that he may bring it to a happy issue. Continue to intercede for me until my request is granted. But above all, obtain for me the grace one day to see my God face to face, and with you and Mary and all the saints to praise and bless him for all eternity. Amen.

Recite the above prayer, followed by the Our Father, Hail Mary, Glory be, and the following invocation to Saint Ann after each day's reflection.

---

[41]   Saint Ann is the mother of the Blessed Virgin Mary, and the patron saint of unmarried women, mothers, and housewives.

Saint Ann, help me now and at the hour of my death! Good Saint Ann, intercede for me!

First Day

Dear Saint Ann, I appeal to you and place myself under your great motherly care as I begin this novena in your honor. Please listen to my prayers and requests. Help me, also, to begin this time of prayer with a heart open to the loving grace of God. Give me the strength to begin a new life that will last forever. Finally, blessed Saint Ann, I ask you to recommend me to your daughter, the most holy virgin Mary. Through her, may I receive the spirit of prayer, humility, and the love of God.

Second Day

From the depths of my heart, good Saint Ann, I offer you my homage and I ask you to shelter me under the mantle of your motherly care. Help me to purify my thoughts and desires.

Aid my decisions that all that I do may be done in love.

Third Day

Good Saint Ann, you were the first to respond to the needs of Mary, the mother of our Savior. You watched over her in her infancy, presented her at the temple, and consecrated her to the service of God. By the great power God has given you, show yourself to be my mother and consoler. Help me dedicate myself to God and to my neighbors. Console me in my trials and strengthen me in my struggles.

Fourth Day

Good Saint Ann, you offered your daughter in the temple with faith, piety, and love. With the happiness which then filled your heart, help me to present myself to God and to the world as a committed disciple of Jesus. Take me under your protection. Strengthen me in my temptations. Show yourself to be a mother and help me to live a life of holiness and love.

Fifth Day

Good Saint Ann, by God's special favor, grant consolation to us who invoke you. Help us to grow in spiritual wealth for the life to come, and guide us in our temporal affairs as well.

Grant us the gift of continuous conversion and renewal of heart. Help us to accept the Gospel of Jesus over and over again so that we may be ready to be true disciples in whatever situations we may experience during our lives.

Sixth Day

Good Saint Ann, free my heart of pride, vanity, and self-love. Help me to know myself as I really am, and to learn meekness and simplicity of heart.

I realize God's great love for me. Help me to reflect this love through works of mercy and charity toward my neighbor.

Seventh Day

Good Saint Ann, by the power and grace God has placed in you, extend to me your helping hand. Renew my mind and heart. I have unbounded confidence in your prayers. Direct my actions according to your goodness and wisdom. I place myself under your motherly care.

Pray that I may receive the grace to lead a devout life on earth, and that I may obtain the everlasting reward of heaven.

Eighth Day

Saint Ann, you gave birth to Mary, whose divine Son brought forth salvation to our world by conquering death and restoring hope to all people. Help me to pray to Him who, for love of us, clothed Himself with human flesh. May I be guided from anything that is displeasing in the sight of God. Pray that the Spirit of Jesus may enlighten and direct me in all I do. Good Saint Ann, keep a watchful eye on me. Help me bear all my crosses, and sustain me with courage.

Ninth Day

Good Saint Ann, I have come to the end of this novena in your honor. Do not let your kind ear grow weary of my prayers, though I repeat them so often. Implore for me from God's providence all the help I need to get through life. May your generous hand bestow on me the material means to satisfy my needs, and to alleviate the plight of the poor. Good Saint Ann, pray that I may praise and thank the Holy Trinity for all eternity.

Chapter 4

Motherhood and Nurturing

"Thank you, women who are mothers! You have
sheltered human beings within yourselves in a unique
experience of joy and travail. This experience makes
you become God's own smile upon the newborn
child, the one who guides your child's first steps,
who helps it to grow, and who is the anchor as the
child makes its way along the journey of life."

—Saint John Paul II

The twentieth century theologian, Yves Congar, in his
treatise, *The Meaning of Tradition,* uses the images of
a father and a mother to explain the difference between
doctrine and tradition in the life of the Church. Doctrine,
he says, has a masculine quality. Not only has the teaching authority of the Church been entrusted to an all-male
clergy and ecclesiastical hierarchy, but the nature of dogmatic teaching is itself masculine in its paternal, authoritative, and logical qualities.

By contrast, tradition has a feminine quality. As Congar explains, "We may even discern a feminine and maternal touch in the vital aspect of tradition. A woman expresses instinctively and vitally what a man expresses logically. The man is the logos, the external agent. The woman is the recipient, the matrix and fashioner of life. She creates the surroundings in which life will retain its warmth; one thinks of the maternal breast, of tenderness, of the home. She is fidelity."[42]

I love this association of mothers and tradition. The traditions of the Church and the traditions of the home impact us on a deep and abiding level. Traditions—the "surroundings in which life will retain its warmth"[43]—are what make a house a home. Real, organic traditions knit a family together because when we participate in them, we repeat a ritual that ties us together in a deeper but not unlike manner, as do house rules for a board game or an inside joke among friends.

Traditions give us a feeling of familiarity, of something expected that puts us at our ease. Think of your family's Christmas traditions. Family tradition dictates that, when we are spending Christmas with my husband's family, everyone comes down the stairs first thing in the morning in the most ridiculous pajamas they own and eats cinnamon rolls under the Christmas tree. By contrast, when we

---

[42]   Yves Congar, *The Meaning of Tradition*. (San Francisco: Ignatius Press, 2004), 24.

[43]   Yves Congar, *The Meaning of Tradition*, 24.

are staying with my family, Christmas morning sees Christmas dresses and suit coats walking out the door for early morning Mass, while the kids (and maybe an adult or two) try to get one good peek at what awaits them under the tree when we get home. In each circumstance, nobody needs to be told what to expect the night before—it is a mark of belonging to the family that we all know what to do.

And the same is true with the Church. Catholics raised organically in the Faith do not need to think about it when we enter a church built faithfully to tradition: Holy Water font by the door. Sign of the Cross. Tabernacle in its traditional spot right up front. Genuflect as we reach our pew. Strip tradition away, and you are left with a bare belief system that demands your intellectual assent without cultivating your emotional, psychological, and spiritual need to belong.

Obviously, you could generalize men as logical versus women as instinctive and nurturing in Yves Congar's metaphor. But it is true that our natures emphasize common human traits differently. Little children know this instinctively: toddlers, with rare exceptions, vastly prefer Mommy when they really need consolation. And statistics overwhelmingly suggest that a father's worldview and religious beliefs impact his children to a greater degree than do their mother's.[44] That is why it is so vital for the two parents to work together.

---

[44] See Polly House, "Want your church to grow? Then bring in the men." Baptist Press, April 3, 2003. https://www.baptistpress.com

But for almost a century, both tradition and home-making have been under attack by a society that does not really see their value. Part of the issue is that the world has sped up—there is just so much we are expected to do and no time to do it in. Slowing down, deliberately cultivating and nurturing the home is hard to do with all the demands upon our time. But there is also the reality that society pushes us women to contribute in ways that vie with male accomplishments. You see this in the demand for women's ordination—women have largely forgotten our traditional role of nurturing the local parish as a home and so many want to co-opt dogmatic male roles.

Without women serving as the "fashioner[s] of life,"[45] nurturing the surroundings for the family and the Church, all of us lose our sense of home. This is one of the biggest crises in the twentieth and twenty-first centuries: home has become less and less concrete, leaving people to feel isolated, disconnected, and alienated from each other and from a necessary sense of place.

/resource-library/news/want-your-church-to-grow-then-bring-in-the-men/. See also Nick Cady. "The Impact on Kids of Dad's Faith and Church Attendance." Nickcady.org. June 20, 2016. https://nickcady.org/2016/06/20/the-impact-on-kids-of-dads-faith-and-church-attendance/.
45 Yves Congar, *The Meaning of Tradition*, 24.

Question

Lots of moms feel like they are pulled in so many different directions—work, school, sports practices, extracurricular activities, events, errands, etc. One of my good friends admitted to me that she resents the push to book up every spare moment with things and activities and yearns to just be home. She worried that it made her come across as selfish—the mom who prioritizes home over experiences and activities. I think that is a common fear a lot of us moms have. And yet we are often drawn toward home, wanting to develop home into more than just the place where we come back to at the end of our events. What are your thoughts?

Answer by Sister Christina, Capuchin Sisters of Nazareth

As the old saying goes, "Home is where the heart is." In our secularized society, we've lost a sense of both the home—where the family is rooted—and the heart—where all love is born.

The mother is the heart of the home. If she's not home, what happens to the heartbeat? The home simply becomes a house.

I recently came across the testimony of a mother who transitioned from a high paying career, traveling the world, to homeschooling her five children. Primed by the culture to believe that the modern-day mother should not stay home, she was eventually touched by

God through a conversation she attributes to the Blessed Mother. What was once seen as a successful career and all the prestige one could hope for left her feeling empty and restless. "I was blinded," she wrote. "God would not allow me to experience rest in my soul when I was so far away from living the truth and fulfilling my true vocation as a wife and mother."

As a mother at home, perhaps you face criticism that you're letting your talents and education go to waste, buried away in your home and tending only to the needs of your children and household. What need could be more pressing than that? Your mission is to cultivate souls for heaven by creating in your home a "little heaven" on earth. You remind your children that it's not about *here* but about *there*!

God created us *to be*, not to do. Your worth, your dignity, is not in what you produce but in who you are. Don't let the world tell you that you are not something—you are someone—a mother!

Allow me to conclude with the words of Joseph Cardinal Mindszenty. His respect for mothers was deep and abiding. He wrote one book entitled *The Mother*, and had planned two more; however, his imprisonment by the Nazis and then the Communists prevented the completion of his work. In that book, he writes:

> The most important person on earth is a mother. She cannot claim the honor of having built Notre Dame Cathedral. She need not. She has built

something more magnificent than any cathe-
dral—a dwelling for an immortal soul, the tiny
perfection of her baby's body . . . the angels have
not been blessed with such a grace. They cannot
share in God's creative miracle to bring new saints
to heaven. Only a human mother can. Mothers are
closer to God the Creator than any other creature;
God joins forces with mothers in performing this
act of creation . . . what on God's good earth is more
glorious than this: to be a mother?[46]

Amen!

Question

The Church is called Mater et Magistra—*Mother and
Teacher. How can Christian women, in our own calling
to be mothers, whether as spiritual mothers or physical
mothers, support the Church in its role as the Bride of
Christ and the mother of all believers?*

Answer by Mother Abbess
Cecilia, Benedictines

I think it is important to understand that motherhood is
written very deeply into the nature of women, whether they
are called to physical motherhood or not. I believe every
woman is called to be a spiritual mother, to meet God

---

[46]   Joseph Cardinal Mindszenty, *The Mother*. Rev. Benedict P. Lenz,
C.Ss.R., Translator (Radio Replies Press, 1949), 65-66.

within her own capacities of giving, nurturing, and sustaining life. A woman is not truly free until she comes to terms with this aspect of how we were created, and how closely we can work with the Creator. So it is that spiritual maternity is the context of all our progress in the spiritual life.

Men must engage their imaginations with ideas of spiritual combat and apostolic mission. However, Holy Mother Church has recognized the innate tendency of women as natural contemplatives, whether in the cloisters of their own *ecclesiola*, the little family of the domestic church, or the cloisters of religious houses. Even active women religious are bound to some degree of separation to nourish within us the maternal instinct to "mother" souls in the very interior of the Church, just as women nurture life physically in their own bodies. So, everyone can really be a spiritual mother by her prayers, by offering sacrifice, and daily works for the children she does not see, but whom she bears by faith.

Prayer excerpted from the Latin Rite Churching of a Woman after Childbirth[47]

V. She shall receive a blessing from the Lord, and mercy from God her Savior: for this is the generation of them that seek the Lord. Enter into the temple of God, adore

---

47   "The Churching of Women." https://www.fisheaters.com/church ingofwomen.html.

the Son of the blessed Virgin Mary, who gave you fruitfulness of offspring. Lord, have mercy. Christ, have mercy. Lord, have mercy. Our Father, who art in heaven. . . .

V. And lead us not into temptation,

R. But deliver us from evil.

V. Save your handmaid, Lord.

R. Who hopes in Thee, my God.

V. Send her help, Lord, from the sanctuary.

R. And defend her out of Sion.

V. Let not the enemy prevail against her.

R. Nor the son of iniquity approach to hurt her.

V. O Lord, hear my prayer.

R. And let my cry come to Thee.

V. The Lord be with you.

R. And with thy spirit.

V. Let us pray: Almighty, everlasting God, through the delivery of the blessed Virgin Mary, Thous hast turned into joy the pains of the faithful in childbirth; look mercifully upon this Thy handmaid, coming in gladness to Thy temple to offer up her thanks: and grant that after this life, by the merits and intercession of the same blessed Mary, she may merit to arrive, together with her offspring, at the joys of everlasting happiness. Through Christ our Lord.

R. Amen.

CHAPTER 5

Sacrifice

"Look at the mothers who truly love their children:
how many sacrifices they make for them. They are
ready for everything, even to give their own blood so
that their babies grow up good, healthy, and strong."

—Saint Gianna Beretta Molla

My husband and I were married according to the
Eastern Rite of marriage. In that ceremony, the
priest crowns the bride and groom with actual crowns
that are tied together by a long ribbon. It is a beautiful,
visual symbol of unity, similar to the old Latin practice of
the priest binding the bride and groom's hands together
in the folds of his priestly stole. However, the Eastern
wedding crowns also symbolize the beginning of our
marital authority as yet-to-be father and mother of our
household. We are crowned in our glorious vocation of
matrimony, vested with the authority of our vocation.

But, as the priest explained to us, these crowns are
also our crowns of martyrdom. When two individuals
become one in the vocation of marriage, we die to self
and to our former unattached freedoms in the world. To

this day, our crowns remind us of our life-long vocational vows. We do not live for ourselves any longer. Many nuns also have a tradition of receiving a crown when they take their vows. Some nuns receive beautiful floral crowns, others, austere crowns of thorns. Traditionally, medieval German nuns wore linen crowns embroidered with crosses. Saint Hildegard von Bingen, a twelfth century monastic and Doctor of the Church, crowned her nuns with crowns of actual gold when they made their professions. Saint Gertrude the Great reflected that this nun's crown was her marriage crown, received when she became the Bride of Christ. Additionally, a newly professed nun's crown, like my marriage crown, is a crown of martyrdom, since by taking her vows, a nun dies to the world and its freedoms.

The term martyr is a tricky word these days, because we tend to think of it as a very foreign term. Most people assume that martyrdom is obsolete in the modern world, though there are pockets in distant lands where Christians are still called upon to die for their faith. Christians in the West are hardly living through anything like the Age of Martyrs in the first few centuries of the Church, where Christians of all ages and classes were tortured and brutally murdered.

When martyrdom is mentioned in connection with cushy modern life with its relative freedoms, you are liable to get an eyeroll or a full-on derisive snort. "Oh, you think you are such a martyr!" is a dismissive refrain—as if comparing our little struggles, sacrifices, persecutions, and oppressions to those of Saint Agnes or Saint Paul is offensive and absurd: "Saint Ignatius of Antioch was eaten alive by a literal lion, and here you are comparing your marriage to a loving spouse with wonderful children to that!"

I am under no illusion that I would make a good martyr—the red martyrdom that we all know from the stories of saints who won their halos through heroic faithfulness at the point of a sword or under the claws of beasts. I cannot stand mice, let alone lions, and I tend to fall into embarrassed silence at social gatherings when I might instead speak up for the truth—and all I have to lose is social comfort! Obviously, physical martyrdom is a thing both vastly more difficult and more worthy of honor, and traditionally, the Church recognized the sainthood of such martyrs without the requirement for miraculous evidence in the canonization process.

But just as we are called upon to imitate the Immaculate Mother of God to the best of our fallen ability, we are also called to humble imitation of the martyrs. This does not mean seeking out literal martyrdom, but rather living out our vocations with sacrificial intent. Historically, the Church has come up with a way of talking about this type of martyrdom. Saint Jerome, writing about the desert ascetic hermits who originated the monastic vocation, described the lifestyle of rigorous sacrifice as a "white martyrdom." Later, an anonymous medieval Irish homily from the seventh century, called the Cambrai Homily, added another type, a "blue martyrdom," sometimes called a "green martyrdom," because Old Irish does not really distinguish between those two colors.[48] It is to this blue martyrdom that all the rest of us Christians are called.

According to the Cambrai Homily, "there are three kinds of martyrdom which are counted as a cross to man, that is to say, white martyrdom, and green (blue) martyrdom, and red martyrdom."[49] Describing the white and blue martyrdoms, the Irish homilist says that the white martyrdom occurs when "man separates for the sake of God from everything he loves," and embarks upon a life of fasting and labor for the Kingdom of Heaven. In other words—the religious vocation! The blue martyrdom, by contrast, is when, "by means of fasting and labor, man separates from his desires, or suffers toil in penance and repentance."[50] Suffering toil—Adam the husband earning his family's bread with the sweat of his brow, and Eve the wife suffering the toil of childbirth: parents, sacrificing their desires for the good of the family.

The difference between the white and the blue martyrdoms is that white is accomplished apart from the world, like a desert hermit or a contemplative monastic, and blue

[48]   "The Three Kinds of Martyrdom from the Cambrai Homily." OmniumSanctorumHibernae.org 2012.
[49]   Whitley Stokes, and John Strachan, editors. *Thesaurus Palaeohibernicus: a collection of Old-Irish glosses, Scholia prose and verse* (Cambridge University Press, 1901), 247.
[50]   Whitley Stokes, and John Strachan, editors. *Thesaurus Palaeohibernicus*, 247.

is achieved in the world, as mothers and fathers are called to do. And while red martyrdom is infinitely special in the Christian understanding, the Cambrai Homily insists that all three kinds of martyrdom "are precious in God's eyes, for which we obtain rewards if we fulfill them."[51]

The hard thing about this sort of martyrdom is that it is a *daily grind* sort of martyrdom, almost a martyrdom by a thousand papercuts! Most days, it is decidedly not a heroic feeling, as we attempt to win our blue crowns of martyrdom by shuffling down the stairs in our slippers, long before we wanted to be awake, to feed the kids and start the day. It is easy to justify the moments where we fail to embrace our crosses because such instances do not particularly look like crosses; in an instant, we find ourselves snapping at our husbands or griping at our kids before we have had a chance to notice the opportunity for grace. Perhaps, we flatter ourselves, if it were only a real lion, we could act like real martyrs. . . .

Question

A lot of women feel pressure to be more than just a mom. These days, our identity seems tied to flashy job titles, and people only know how to measure success in terms of salaries, promotions, and resume lines. Stay-at-home mothers especially face the criticism that we are letting our talents and education go to waste, buried away in our

---

[51] Whitley Stokes, and John Strachan, editors. *Thesaurus Palaeohibernicus*, 247.

homes and tending only to the needs of our households and children. Sometimes, it is tempting to give in to this sort of pressure. As a nun, you too have chosen to step outside of society's measure of success. How would you counsel a mother who is struggling with nagging fears or criticism that she is wasting her skills at home?

Answer by Mother Mary Angela and the Roswell Poor Clares

We discussed this question in community and had a wonderful conversation!

The first suggestion was simply: look to Our Lady for a model. The Mother of God, the greatest woman who ever lived, was content to live a hidden life in Nazareth, caring for Jesus and Joseph with no worldly attention or success ever expected or desired. She was surely also the most intelligent woman who ever lived, given her intellect untouched by original sin. And she used it very happily and contentedly, we may be sure, in the service of her family. Did any stay-at-home mother in history have more to do with the salvation of the world?

A large issue in this question is boundaries. Who decides what a woman should do? The neighbors? Relatives who want to see this person succeed according to their own standards and ideas? Well-intentioned but interfering friends? We must be firm in our own values and convictions and not allow worldly values or opinions to influence our decisions. In the end, to whom do we look for approval? A woman has to believe in what she is called to do and believe in her own individual vocation. Our neighbors and relatives will not be responsible before God for our choices and decisions, and it is not up to them to determine the vocation to which God calls us, nor the way in which we will carry it out.

Both in the cloister and in family life, our creative talents and our intelligence can be very well-used—to the maximum! What greater responsibility is there than to be entrusted with the formation and welfare of a human soul, which is of infinite value? What could be more challenging, what could possibly call forth more creative effort and energy than making a home a happy place to live, helping one's children flourish and deepening one's relationship of love with one's spouse? We know the old maxim: "The hand that rocks the cradle rules the world." Raising children well is an enormous investment in the world's welfare. We can change the culture, one child at a time.

Another important issue that this question raises is the understanding of the value of sacrifice. It may well be that a woman is called to sacrifice her career, and all that it may have held in the way of self-fulfillment, to respond more fully to the vocation of wife and mother. If this sacrifice is made freely and with a loving heart, it is an admirable and powerful thing, which will certainly bear fruit in the life of the family.

We also want to question the idea that we are required to fulfill ourselves to the utmost and use all our talents to the maximum. This idea can be somewhat tyrannical—the tyranny of the talents! Also, this idea is simply not possible (and perhaps not necessarily desirable) in any vocation. The best use of a gift might well be to make a sacrifice of it. We do have to learn, over time, to focus on the things that really matter, the most important things that pertain to our own vocation. And when we are steadfast in our own values over time, the so-called values of the world lose their attraction.

It was also pointed out in our community conversation that this issue should be discussed before marriage: what are the priorities—the wife's career or raising children? Thus, it becomes the shared decision of the couple, with the best interests of all in mind.

Question

When you're exhausted, perhaps lonely, and the work is piling up, do you ever have trouble staying motivated? If yes, how do you push through?

Answer by Mother Abbess Cecilia, Benedictines

Exhaustion is a typical symptom in monastic life, and it cannot always be helped except by the very simple remedy of sleep. Saint Thomas Aquinas speaks of the usefulness of a hot bath and sleep as a remedy for sorrow in the *Summa*. This is, as is St. Thomas, very wise! It is not good to depend on creature comforts, but the strain of a life of sacrifice—which includes heavy demands upon the mind, heart, and soul—means there should be corresponding joys for healthy equilibrium. This is why St. Ignatius is adamant that meals should taste good and that we must have periods of recreation, that is, the hour in which we are permitted to break silence and speak freely. While having sisters in community is not a substitute for having our own families, it is a compensation from the Lord to strengthen us in our vocation.

In the meantime, we often think of the sacrifice of mothers to keep us going, thinking of their vigils and sacrifices. This is a major motivation, because we know we have a great amount of spiritual children in need of care. In our case, the idea is shepherding souls into eternal life, begging God for the graces to touch them, entering in where no human has power, and giving grace to convert hearts.

If confidence in God or loving feelings of consolation fail, it is where the "hellfire and brimstone" comes in handy. Thinking of eternity, an eternity of suffering or of bliss, is one of the best ways to get the soul moving again. We do not want to emphasize fear too much, but St. Benedict says fear of the Lord is the beginning of wisdom, and this is exactly why. Healthy fear of the Lord, which is a gift of the Holy Ghost, leads to wisdom, that is, seeing things as God sees them.

We often need a healthy dose of fear to get out of ourselves and back to loving God, who is the reason we came to religious life, and to immerse ourselves in it once more with thanksgiving. We do not want to displease Him or let

Him down, but to fling ourselves on His Mercy with confidence. At the same time, we want to let that same action fling us forward into whatever tasks He gives us to make up for what is wanting. He really is so kind in giving us so many opportunities to set ourselves straight and be generous with Him again. When a soul is generous and in love, it is then most truly wise and where God wants it to be.

Question

How do you sanctify the mundane? How do you keep Christ at the center of your day when you are at work doing everyday tasks?

Answer by Mother Mary Angela and the Roswell Poor Clares

There were many suggestions from our community in response to this question, most of them simple and practical, and I will offer them in the form of suggestions:

- Begin the day with a Morning Offering.
- Make an actual place in the home for prayer, a little corner or other place, perhaps with a small table or altar on which holy images, statues, and Sacred Scripture can be placed. Holy images and good sacred art on the walls of the home will also help to call spiritual realities to mind. This could also be a place where the family prays together.
- Singing and humming religious songs to oneself at

daily tasks is enjoyable and helpful.

- Strive to practice the presence of God throughout the day—many spiritual directors encourage the practice of offering a special aspiration or other prayer at the striking of the clock (if you have a clock that strikes!), or when moving from room to room in the house—just some prayer that will recall the memory of God's presence to our minds and hearts.
- Offer certain actions for determined intentions. For example, when preparing the meal or washing the dishes, pray in gratitude that there was food to prepare and enjoy. When we accomplish our tasks as a part of our vocation to homemaking, we do the will of God. It helps to be deliberate about it, to embrace it as part of His perfect will, His loving design for us, and to believe that the difficult things will help us grow, mature, and become the saints He wants us to be!
- Simply pray the Holy Name of Jesus and other aspirations throughout the day. Also, ask Our Lady, guardian angels, patron saints, or our favorite saints for help throughout the day.
- Even a few minutes of reading from the Sacred Scriptures or a good spiritual book can give us something to think about as we do our manual work.
- One of our Christian doctors told us, "I just want to be a channel of God's love to each person." What a beautiful inspiration for a wife and mother!

An additional note:
In the book, *Strange Gods Before Me,* Mother Mary Francis writes with wit and wisdom about the accusation that young women are "wasting their talents" by entering the cloister. This can be found in the chapter on "The Surface God." It might be very good reading in reference to this question.

A reflection on sacrifice according to the Little Way of Saint Therese of Lisieux, from a letter to her sister[52]

We must not let slip one single occasion of sacrifice, everything has such value in the religious life . . . Pick up a pin from a motive of love, and you may thereby convert a soul. Jesus alone can make our deeds of such worth, so let us love Him with every fiber of our heart.

---

[52]   Saint Therese of Lisieux. *The Story of a Soul: The Autobiography of St. Therese of Lisieux.* Thomas N. Taylor, Translator. Project Gutenberg Ebook. September 28, 2005. https://www.gutenberg.org/cache /epub/16772/pg16772-images.html.

CHAPTER 6

Isolation and Solitude

"Behold, an angel of the Lord appeared to Joseph in a
dream and said, 'Rise, take the child and his mother,
and flee to Egypt, and remain there till I tell you.'"

—Mt 2:13

I cannot help but think how incredibly lonely Mary
must have felt in Egypt. Not only did she have to cope
with giving birth in an inhospitable stable in Bethlehem,
away from her family, friends, and all the comforts of
home, but now she and Joseph were ripped away from
their very culture. And for how long? The angel never
gave them a concrete timeline.

There were probably many, many days where Mary
never talked to another adult until Joseph came in late
from whatever work he had managed to find that day. If
Joseph was anything like my husband, there were probably a few days where he was just too burnt out to be very
social. While Mary was blessed with the literal, physical
presence of God in her house, her Lord and Savior was
still a little baby. We can't know what the infant Jesus

was really like, but for us, even a very precocious and
well-behaved baby is still a baby whose needs for food,
rest, and cleaning up are endless. I imagine that she may
have longed, at times, for conversation with the crowd of
village girls back home with whom Our Lady must have
enjoyed laughing and talking, or the older women in her
family who were sociably busy about the house.

Isolation is the struggle that most mothers, no matter
their age or stage in motherhood, have had to face. Modern mothers in particular face alarming rates of isolation.
A 2021 study calculated that 51% of mothers of young
children are deeply lonely—a sad reality that was exacerbated, but not caused, by the lockdowns of 2020.[53] Part of
it is due to the fact that modern moms often find themselves living far away from extended family, and the old
village community that Mother Mary must have missed
in Egypt has never existed for most of us in our sprawl-
ing, dehumanized cities and suburbs.

But isolation also seems baked into the vocation of
motherhood. The natural division of labor in family life
means that us mothers often find ourselves at home,
away from typical adult social interactions. While children have a deep need for both their father and mother,
young children need their mother's physical presence and

[53]   Richard Weissbourd, Milena Batanova, Virginia Lovison, and
Eric Torres, "Loneliness in America How the Pandemic Has Deep-
ened an Epidemic of Loneliness and What We Can Do About It." Har-
vard Graduate School of Education. 2021. https://mcc.gse.harvard
.edu/reports/loneliness-in-america.

nurturing role in a way that often limits mothers' ability to engage with the world outside the home. After all, for those of us mothers who received the great blessing of being able to nurse our children, nobody can attend to that great, urgent task other than ourselves. This reality puts a severe restriction upon what we can do outside the home. In addition, all mothers must sacrifice their social lives and interests for the sake of toddler naps, children's bedtimes, school schedules, and routines.

When you think about it, the sort of isolation that mothers encounter is, in some ways, like that of the cloister. It is part of our vocation to step away from the world to fulfill the divine task to which we have been called. Our isolation is also, like that of the cloistered nun, in loving service to a community: both the little community of the convent or the family and to the greater communities of our Church, our nation, and our world.

Question

Recently, I found myself at an extended family reunion. My little children were exhausted and one of us—my husband or myself—needed to stay in the hotel room with them and miss out on quality adult time with our family. Of course, with a nursing baby, the choice was obvious, and I spent many long hours that night in the dark, coaxing little ones to go to sleep. It struck me that mothers of little children have a sort of "movable cloister." We go all sorts of places but are very restricted in our interaction with the world outside the needs of our little ones. I was very disappointed to be missing the fun evening downstairs in the lobby but ended up meditating on the fact that, for nuns, the cloister is not an inconvenience that you must deal with, but an aspect of your vocation which you seek out. Please share with me some wisdom you have gained from embracing the limitations and constraints that are part of your vocation.

Answer by Mother Mary Angela and the Roswell Poor Clares

Those restrictions are actually freeing! They focus us more on God and His will for us, on where we are, and what we are doing. "In God's will is our peace." We are more able to be present in the present moment. One sister said, "This is what I am called to do, and it frees me from all the other things that would be possible."

In the example given, the opportunity was there to embrace the sacrifice of missing out on the family inter-action downstairs and to make the choice to joyfully and intentionally be with the little ones that needed love and care. This is not to say that we will not *feel* the sacrifice—we will, and we do—but we did make the sacrifice, and we are given opportunities (such as this one) to intentionally offer it again.

Part of maturity is knowing what our responsibili-ties are, what we should be doing, and where our duty lies: Putting our children first, rather than ourselves, not longing to be somewhere else when duty calls us "here," and remembering that God has a way of compensating us for the sacrifices we make—although we don't sacrifice expecting a compensation!

It is good to remember that sacrifice flows from love and is always fruitful. In the example given, it was surely fruitful both for the children who experienced the care of their mother and the family downstairs who understood the mother's choice to put her children first. She witnessed to her belief in her own vocation to motherhood. Additionally, there is the reality that children grow up very quickly, therefore, time with them is precious, even if it requires sacrifice.

One of the sisters mentioned the beautiful passage from *Verbi Sponsa*, the document on cloistered contemplative life from the Vatican. Below is an excerpt that she specifically mentioned:

> 3. In a specific and radical way, cloistered contemplatives conform to Christ Jesus in prayer on the mountain and to his Paschal Mystery, which is death for the sake of resurrection. (10) . . .
>
> This association of the contemplative life with the prayer of Jesus in a solitary place suggests a unique way of sharing in Christ's relationship with the Father. The Holy Spirit, who led Jesus into the desert (cf. *Lk* 4:1), invites the nun to share the solitude of Christ Jesus, who "with the eternal Spirit" (*Heb* 9:14) offered himself to the Father. The solitary cell, the closed cloister, are the place where

the nun, bride of the Incarnate Word, lives wholly concentrated with Christ in God. The mystery of this communion is revealed to her to the extent that, docile to the Holy Spirit and enlivened by his gifts, she listens to the Son (cf. *Mt* 17:5), fixes her gaze upon his face (cf. *2 Cor* 3:18), and allows herself to be conformed to his life, to the point of the supreme self-offering to the Father (cf. *Phil* 2:5 ff.), for the praise of his glory.

The enclosure therefore, even in its physical form, is a special way of being with the Lord, of sharing in "Christ's emptying of himself by means of a radical poverty, expressed in . . . renunciation not only of things but also of "space", of contacts, of so many benefits of creation", (12) at one with the fruitful silence of the Word on the Cross. It is clear then that "withdrawal from the world in order to dedicate oneself in solitude to a more intense life of prayer is nothing other than a special way of living and expressing the Paschal Mystery of Christ". (13) It is a true encounter with the Risen Lord, a journey in ceaseless ascent to the Father's house.

In watchful waiting for the Lord's return, the cloister becomes a response to the absolute love of God for his creature and the fulfillment of his eternal desire to welcome the creature into the mystery of intimacy with the Word, who gave himself as Bridegroom in the Eucharist (14) and remains in the tabernacle as the heart of full communion with him, drawing to himself the entire life of the cloistered nun in order to offer it constantly to the Father (cf. *Heb* 7:25). To the gift of Christ the Bridegroom, who on the Cross offered his body unreservedly, the nun responds in like terms with the gift of the "body", offering herself with Jesus Christ to the Father and cooperating with him in the work of redemption. Separation from the world thus gives a Eucharistic quality to the whole of cloistered life, since "besides its elements of sacrifice and expiation, [it assumes] the aspect of thanksgiving to the Father, by sharing in the thanksgiving of the beloved Son". (15)[54]

The cloistered nun can be truly happy without a lot of things, and find true contentment without a lot of things, whether entertainment, commodities, etc.

Personally, I still recall one moment in my life, similar to the one described in the question. My younger sister was getting married, and I still remember my feelings the afternoon of the wedding. It was a poignant experience, because if I had not been cloistered, I would certainly have attended her wedding. But I knew that, as a cloistered contemplative nun, I had renounced that

---

[54] Congregation for Institutes of Consecrated Life and for Societies of Apostolic Life. *Verbi Sponsa*, May 13, 1999. https://www.vatican.va/roman_curia/congregations/ccscrlife/documents/rc_con_ccscrlife_doc_13051999_verbi-sponsa_en.html.

possibility for the love of Christ, and that I indeed would not belong there, had I gone. In faith, I could firmly believe that the sacrifice of not being present for her wedding was far more precious a gift than my physical presence would have been. Even though I fully felt the sacrifice of not being there for the great family occasion, I was deeply at peace.

Question

Study after study suggests that modern mothers overwhelmingly suffer from isolation. I know this is something that I struggle with myself: motherhood means that we are often home alone with small children, far away from family and friends. We often have a hard time relating to single friends but are also too busy with children to easily develop friendships with other mothers. There have been entire days where I end up having no adult conversations except the few moments with my husband at the end of the day. Do nuns struggle at times with isolation and loneliness? How do you cope with it?

Answer by Sister Anne Marie, Cistercians of the Valley of Our Lady

Isolation . . . Does some of the real, painful part of this struggle arise in me from a stance that has, at least a little bit, a tinge of self-pity? Recognizing this can be a very good step toward rooting it out. I might ask myself: Am I open to the possibility that the growth in true holiness coming to me from the loneliness I experience is exactly the holiness God desires for me? Not some other kind of holiness, but this true holiness coming to me from God to expand my capacity for greater and greater love. You mothers may have days with little or no adult conversations; nuns may (and often do) have days lived in a silence in which the gift of aridity in prayer is their food. Are we able to see the Holy Spirit deeply and secretly at work in us? Are we able to *accept* this with a peaceful mind and heart? Could God be calling me to place on the altar of sacrifice my self-centered hankering for a personal fulfillment of my own making?

Question

Do you ever get bored fulfilling your vocation? I love my children and delight in being a mother . . . but there are those days where it is just so boring. When people see all my little kids running around, they like to smile and say, "never a dull moment in your house!" But there are quite a few of them! How do you handle boredom in your vocation?

Answer by Mother Abbess
Cecilia, Benedictines

Boredom is a funny thing; it does not necessarily mean a lack of activity. Most mothers and nuns prefer a lack of activity, or a lack of social engagements. I think most of us who love our vocations will find ourselves as homebodies, even if peace and quiet is always an elusive dream.

Nevertheless, in the downtimes, or in simple ennui, we often come in contact with ourselves, our insecurity, and what is lacking in us before God. Silence is appalling to modern man, and we try to clutter it up as soon as possible to crowd out the image of ourselves, the image which we remain: the image and likeness of God.

Boredom might follow, because if we lose interest in the pursuit of God and prefer other amusements to Him, we will quickly see their emptiness and our weakness. The real solution to boredom is prayer, a deep relationship with Christ, walking with Him every day. If He takes such great interest in our lives, we should not lose it. So rather than turning to things other than the "normal," a good strategy is to thrill in the normal and in the daily duty.

A beautiful spokesman of this is G. K. Chesterton. He wrote extensively on glorying in our lot, saying among other things:

> A child kicks his legs rhythmically through excess, not absence, of life. Because children have abounding vitality, because they are in spirit fierce and free, therefore they want things repeated and unchanged. They always say, 'Do it again' … Perhaps God is strong enough to exult in monotony. It is possible that God says every morning, 'Do it again' to the sun; and every evening, 'Do it again' to the moon. It may not be automatic necessity that makes all daisies alike; it may be that God makes

every daisy separately, but he never got tired of making them. It may be that He has the eternal appetite of infancy; for we have sinned and grown old, and our Father is younger than we. The repetition in Nature may not be a mere recurrence; it may be a theatrical encore.[55]

In the end, we must see that the very things that bore us are part of the road that leads us where we are truly going, to heaven and to eternal life. Even if life is missing some excitement, it has the merit of being the means to an end so wonderful that we cannot begin to dream it: "What no eye has seen, nor ear heard, nor the heart of man conceived, what God has prepared for those who love him."[56] This love is shown in little ways, even in the things that strike us as boring. Signposts can be very boring, but if we see them for what they are, they become very useful.

Answer by Sister Colette, Capuchin Sisters of Nazareth

In any vocation, life can tend to be monotonous. As human beings, we desire what is new and exciting. With God, everything is new because He gives us a share in His divine nature. No matter how many times you mop the floor or do a load of laundry, it is always a

---

[55]   G.K. Chesterton, *Orthodoxy* (Image Books, New York: 1959), 60.
[56]   1 Cor 2:9.

new action and a new opportunity to share in Christ's redeeming work. Imagine how many times Our Lady hauled water from the well, stoked the fire, or set the table for dinner. She was always glad to do it, because in doing every action for and with Jesus, she was saving souls. When preoccupied with saving souls through the offering of prayer and works, how can life be boring?

But the reality for many religious is that sometimes life does become a routine. In these times, it takes a heroic soul to start fresh. In the words of Saint Maximilian Kolbe, "only love is creative."[57] When I find the monotony of our schedule dull, I am inspired by reading the biography of a saint to see how they grew in holiness and love of God. When prayer is dry, I try a new devotional practice like devotion to the Seven Sorrows of Our Lady, or the invocation of the Jesus Prayer, or prayers for the souls in purgatory. It could be anything to spice up the relationship and rekindle the fire of God's love in one's vocation. Let the Lord lead you, because the last thing He would want is for you to feel boredom and loneliness. He wants boredom to be united back to Him with peace.

---

[57]   Patricia Treece, *A Man for Others: Maximilian Kolbe the "Saint of Auschwitz in the Words of Those Who Knew Him,"* (Libertyville: Marytown, 1982), 188.

A Prayer in Special Time of Need to Our Lady of Consolation[58]

Mary, Loving Mother of Consolation, I turn to you now in this time of need. I come to you confused and fearful, anxious as a little child.

I know you really are my Mother. You see me with eyes filled with love and understanding. Touch me through your prayers and hold me in your love, that I might continue strong and unafraid in these days of difficulty and hurt.

Gentle Mother, I now confide to you my greatest need (pause and reflect). Please pray that the loving will of Our Father may always come first in my heart and in my mind.

Help me to reflect on the needs in your own life, Mary, the days when you, too, knew concern, fear, loneliness, and grief. You always turned to Our Father and gave yourself to Him completely. You knew His love and showed us how to live in it.

When I remember the love of your Blessed Son for me, I am less afraid. When I think of you, I can smile. Pray for me, Mary. Guide me always in your love, and lead me to your Son, Jesus. Amen.

---

[58]   From the National Shrine of Our Lady of Consolation in Carey, Ohio. https://www.olcshrine.com/prayers/8-pray/prayers-novenas-honoring -our-lady-of-consolation/10-a-prayer-in-special-time-of-need.

CHAPTER 7

Obedience

"Wives, be subject to your husbands, as to the Lord. For the husband is the head of the wife as Christ is the head of the church, his body, and is himself its Savior."

—Eph 5: 22–23

When Princess Diana married the future King Charles, she made waves by altering the traditional marriage vows of the Anglican Church, editing out the wife's promise to obey her new husband. The world was thrilled—what a giant step forward for women everywhere! After all, we are reminded endlessly, well-behaved women rarely make history. . .

Obedience has such a bad name these days. We want our dogs to obey us, and we send them to obedience training, but other than that, obedience is an increasingly dirty word in polite society. Popular psychology discourages us even from teaching our children to obey. I stumbled across an article the other day that scolded me for wanting the "convenience" of a child who obeys his or her parents. Obedient children, the article informed me, make mindlessly obedient adults who cannot stick up for themselves or lead fulfilling, independent lives. In fact, I was told, teaching obedience is rather immoral—as it prioritizes the act of obeying over the rational decision-making process necessary to determine right action. By contrast, the article concluded, we should celebrate our children when they mouth off to us, because we know that they are turning into confident individuals who can stand up for themselves. Cooperation and negotiation, rather than obedience, are the true virtues.

But the Church has a long history with obedience. Saint Francis de Sales wrote that, "obedience is a virtue of so excellent a nature, that Our Lord was pleased to mark its observance upon the whole course of His life; thus, He often says, He did not come to do His Own will, but that of His Heavenly Father."[59] And just think of it—the only thing we know about the thirty quiet years Jesus spent at home with his mother Mary and foster father Joseph is that He was obedient to His parents.[60] Saint Paul highlights obedience as the central element to Christ's sacrifice on the cross: "And being found in human form he humbled himself and became obedient unto death, even death on a cross."[61] Just as a single act of disobedience caused the fall of the human race, an act of perfect obedience

---

[59] A Parish Priest, "The Teachings of the Saints in their Own Words," as taken from *The Catholic Church, the Teacher of Mankind.* 1905.
[60] See Lk 2:51–2.
[61] Phil 2:8.

saved it: "For as by one man's disobedience many were made sinners, so also by one Man's obedience many will be made righteous."[62]

Obedience has long been praised as the greatest of all offerings to God. Samuel the prophet tells us, "Has the Lord as great delight in burnt offerings and sacrifices, as in obeying the voice of the Lord? Behold, to obey is better than sacrifice, and to hearken than the fat of rams."[63] In other words, the other things we can offer up to God are just that—other things. Offering up our own will in an act of obedience is the most intimate, self-denying sacrifice we can possibly offer.

In fact, the great theologian, Saint Thomas Aquinas, argues that "All virtuous acts belong to obedience insofar as they are done in response to commands. Therefore, Gregory (the Great) says that obedience sows all the virtues in our mind and preserves them insofar as virtuous acts operate causally or dispositively to generate and preserve virtues."[64] What a statement! Firstly, Aquinas is telling us that obedience must come first, because it makes everything else we do pleasing to God. Secondly, Aquinas is telling us that obedience, that humble, difficult, and even humiliating act, makes us like God. The

---

[62]   Rom 5:19.
[63]   1 Samuel 15:22.
[64]   Thomas Aquinas, *On Law, Morality, and Politics*, Second Edition. William P. Baumgarth and Richard J. Regan, editors. Richard J. Regan, translator. (Hackett Publishing Company, Inc: Indianapolis /Cambridge, 2002), 179.

very promise that the devil made to Eve if she disobeyed, "you will be like God,"[65] actually comes through obedience itself.

"Hold up," you say. We have been talking about obedience to God. Of course, that is good, proper, holy. Nobody is contesting that! But what about that harder thing: obeying your husband? Or insisting upon obedience in our children despite the world's disapprobation? Isn't that a bit different?

And yet, Saint Paul, in that oh-so-awkward passage of inspired Scripture, instructs wives to be obedient to our husbands. Of course, as everyone is quick to note, Saint Paul also said that husbands should love their wives as Christ loves the Church—laying down his life for her.[66] Often, I feel, people bring up this bit about what husbands should do to deflect from the fact that wives are specifically called to obey our husbands. Modern folks, Christians included, are just so uncomfortable with that idea. Yes, of course Saint Paul said that our husbands should imitate Christ and lay down their lives for us, but it seems we still owe them holy obedience. Saint Paul didn't say that we only owed them that *if* they managed to get their Christ-like role down perfectly.

Monastics, too, take a vow of obedience. In fact, it is a vow that shows up in all monastic orders, no matter what their charism is and no matter what other vows they take.

---

[65]   Gn 3:5.
[66]   See Ephesians 5.

Not only does a nun vow to obey God and the Church, but she also vows to obey her superiors in the monastery. Obedience seems to be a fundamental part of vocation. Perhaps our modern discomfiture with this perennial virtue needs to be reconsidered.

Question

Obedience plays such a huge role in my life as a mom. I am always focused on teaching my children obedience and expect it from them in so many areas. I must admit, it gets frustrating at times when they struggle to obey, and I often end up taking their failures personally. As a Mother Superior, you are also owed obedience. How should we understand this authority given to us in a way that is both humble and charitable?

Answer by Sister Anne Marie, Cistercians of the Valley of Our Lady

The authority held by a mother for her children and by a religious superior for her sisters is *not* her authority. Rather, it is Christ's authority. It is amazing to think of God and His humility in His willingness to be given to His children through these weak and sinful creatures (mothers and superiors) whom He has chosen to represent Him. Keeping in mind that it is Christ's authority we hold and administer can help us exercise it with proper detachment from a kind of self-importance.

In turn, this helps us lovingly absorb the pain of the failures in obedience that will and do occur. It helps us do this with greater patience, humility, and charity. All the same, disobedience does, most often, need to be *corrected*. Correct with kind words of instruction, giving in this instruction motivation for why they should want to obey. Help them see the lack of peace they experience when they have disobeyed. Correct with love; try to avoid scolding and a tone of voice that goes with scolding.

If you lose your patience and speak more harshly than is good, then apologize a little later for your slip-up. You are not a bad mom because from time to time you lose your patience and react in anger. Your apology is also a way of teaching and guiding your children, because they need to learn how to apologize. Allowing your children to see that you can accept your slip-up (your failure) and that, by turning to Jesus for forgiveness, you can maintain your own peace of mind and heart is important; it is another lesson they need to learn from you.

Question

In the married vocation, obedience has a bad name these days. Wives being submissive to our husbands is not a popular idea, even among more conservative Catholics. As a nun, you have taken a vow of obedience. What is the proper way to think of obedience within the context of vocation?

Answer by Mother Mary Angela and the Roswell Poor Clares

Obedience is a response of love. Love is defined as a union of wills, and when you love someone, you want to do what they desire. Obedience in married life and obedience in religious life are going to differ in that the human spouse is not omniscient, whereas the Divine Spouse is! So, there will definitely be different dynamics involved.

In married life, the ideal is mutual obedience; it would be a matter of giving and receiving, with the desire to honor and respect the other person's needs and wishes. Our Poor Clare Constitutions speak of "obeying the needs of the sisters." The text continues, "For our founders wished us to be humble and subject to all, serving and obeying one another in a spirit of charity. Thus, St. Francis called obedience 'the sister of charity,' and saw in it as well the purest expression of poverty."

Obedience is not meant, surely, to be a matter of one spouse commanding the other from a position of power, but one of mutual understanding. When parts of chapter five of the Letter to the Ephesians are read at Holy Mass, often the whole section about the man laying down his life for the woman is left out—if a man is called to love his wife as his very self, that sets the bar pretty high in regard to respect for her!

Christ wants to continue His life in each of us; He wants to perpetuate His incarnation, His mysteries, in us. He became obedient unto death; He assumed the form of a slave, a servant. His life was all obedience: "My food is to do the will of him who sent me."[67] But this really goes beyond our human strength to imitate; therefore, we have to let Him live His life in us.

Pope St. John Paul II taught us about the "law of the gift" in the Theology of the Body. From this, we learn that we are called to give ourselves as gift.

In our discussion, several sisters mentioned the value of being open with one another in marriage, taking the time necessary to come to an understanding in charity of one another's needs and wishes. It takes time to establish this understanding, and each one must learn to accede generously, with respect and charity. Also, clarity as to which spouse makes what decisions helps.

The present confusion of male identity makes it even more complicated; the man perhaps will need to learn how to be in charge. Genuine submission of the part of the wife means that the husband has to take seriously his responsibility to "command."

Obedience is a sacrifice, whether in marriage or religious life; we renounce our own will, and it is a sacrifice. Often the most precious use of a talent or gift is to offer it in sacrifice.

---

[67]   Jn 4:34.

Question

Why is obedience holy? Why is there such an insistence upon it? It seems rather childish at times . . . something you should be able to grow out of. And yet the Church venerates it so much. Why?

Answer by Sister Joseph, Capuchin Sisters of Nazareth

Obedience is holy because Jesus was obedient to the Father's Will, and it was through His obedient acceptance of the suffering of the cross that salvation came to mankind. The Church teaches that when we are obedient to the Will of God for us, we are then being conformed more and more to Jesus Christ. Additionally, conformity to Jesus Christ is our ultimate vocation and the summit of holiness for every person because conformity to Jesus means conformity to God, and we were created to be in communion—in conformity—with God.

Every human being was created to know and to love God. Furthermore, Scripture teaches us that, ultimately, to love God means to keep His commandments. So, at the moment that we are obedient to Him, we are living to the fullest our identity and vocation as human beings created in the image and likeness of God. We cannot love God and become holy if we are not obedient to Him in our own state of life, which is why there is such an insistence upon obedience by the Church and why the Church venerates it so much.

Contrary to what the world seems to think, obedience is not just a childish virtue to be cultivated in children, or a sign that you cannot think for yourself. In reality, it is when we choose to say yes to God that we are set free from sin.

Question

Why do vocations require obedience? Why do monastics have a vow of obedience and wives—traditionally—owe obedience to our husbands? Is obedience a necessary part of vocation?

Answer by Mother Abbess Cecilia, Benedictines

Obedience seems to be such a naughty word, calling up an image of servility. But two phrases of scripture stand out: He "was obedient to them,"[68] and Christ "became obedient unto death, even death on a cross."[69] The first spells out the humility involved in Christ's obedience. It is true that Christ is regarded as higher than the people in His life like St. Joseph, Our Lady, and even Pilate, but He places Himself under people to show us the "good of obedience," as St. Benedict calls it. Of course, it hurts our fallen, prideful wills to have somebody tell us what to do, especially if they are inferior or do not seem to know what they are doing. But the loving thing to do is

[68]   Lk 2:51.
[69]   Phil 2:8.

to submit and to embrace the sufferings that that might bring. Doing so is *redemptive* if it is done with love.

The Latin for obedience is *ob-audio*. *Audio* means to listen, but *ob* is an intensifier, giving the impression of standing ready, as if in the doorway, ready to do whatever is asked. This is the true spirit of obedience, not only to conform to, but embrace God's will from the heart, especially as expressed by a legitimate superior.

Excerpts from *Introduction to the Devout Life* by Saint Francis de Sales, Doctor of the Church[70]

Love alone leads to perfection, but the three chief means for acquiring it are obedience, chastity, and poverty. Obedience is a consecration of the heart, chastity of the body, and poverty of all worldly goods to the Love and Service of God. These are the three members of the Spiritual Cross, and all three must be raised upon the fourth, which is humility.

Therefore do you obey your superior's commands as of right, but if you would be perfect, follow their counsels, and even their wishes as far as charity and prudence will allow: obey as to things acceptable; as when they bid you eat, or take recreation, for although there may be no great

---

[70] Saint Francis de Sales, "On Obedience" from *Introduction to the Devout Life*. Christian Classics Ethereal Library. https://www.ccel.org/ccel/desales/devout_life.v.xi.html.

virtue in obedience in such a case, there is great harm in disobedience. Obey in things indifferent, as concerning questions of dress, coming and going, singing or keeping silence, for herein is a very laudable obedience. Obey in things hard, disagreeable and inconvenient, and therein lies a very perfect obedience. Moreover, obey quietly, without answering again, promptly, without delay, cheerfully, without reluctance; and above all, render a loving obedience for His Sake Who became obedient even to the death of the Cross for our sake; Who, as Saint Bernard says, chose rather to resign His Life than his Obedience.

If you would acquire a ready obedience to superiors, accustom yourself to yield to your equals, giving way to their opinions where nothing wrong is involved, without arguing or peevishness; and adapt yourself easily to the wishes of your inferiors as far as you reasonably can, and forbear the exercise of stern authority so long as they do well.

It is a mistake for those who find it hard to pay a willing obedience to their natural superiors to suppose that if they were professed religious they would find it easy to obey.

Blessed indeed are the obedient, for God will never permit them to go astray.

CHAPTER 8

Charism, Difference, and Judgement

"To each is given the manifestation of the Spirit for the
common good. . . . *All these are inspired by one and the same
Spirit, who apportions to each one individually as he wills.*"

—1 Cor 12:7, 11

I was once in a conversation with an elderly woman
whose children's children are older than I am. She said,
"When I was doing all this," meaning the time she spent
raising her children, "there wasn't all this fuss about what
type of parent you were. We were all just parents. Everyone did everything basically the same way and had the
same expectations for our children. Not at all like now!"

Not being a historian of parenting styles throughout
the millennia, I have no idea if her perception is actually
true in the aggregate. It is possible there have always been
a few disagreements about the best way to raise kids, but
who knows whether the differences were big enough
to merit their own parenting name and dedicated blog
spaces in decades and centuries past. But I rather think

that the sheer amount of parenting styles—not to mention the associated pressure, guilt, and judgment involved in choosing your parenting identity—has become vastly more intense over the past few decades.

Discussing parenting styles with fellow moms is often stressful. Stressful for me because I must watch how I describe my method of parenting very carefully, lest I scandalize or offend someone who professes a radically different approach. I am always putting my foot in my mouth when I give my opinions about how and when to discipline, grant autonomy or screen time, handle bedtime routines and chore schedules . . . you name it. And I know I am not alone. I have a good friend who visibly freezes up whenever parenting styles are mentioned—she has been on the defensive far too often.

Now, I am not talking smack about parenting styles. Obviously, there are styles out there that are better or worse than others, and we all probably have strong opinions about which ones those are! But I have learned a lot from deeply committed Montessori-style households, I have been inspired by authoritative parents whose houses seem to run like well-oiled machines, and I have been reassured by the "free range" moms who preach unschooling.

In fact, parenting styles are a bit like monastic traditions—there is not one perfect way to be a parent, just like no one religious order has a monopoly on the best system of living out the monastic life. Benedictines, Poor

Clares, Carmelites, Cistercians, Capuchins—these are all different monastic styles that are getting to the same goal: holiness within the context of a contemplative vocation.

The other thing about traditional monastic charisms is that there is not the angst surrounding them like there is around modern parenting styles. A Benedictine and a Poor Clare do not typically feel threatened by each other, even though they have very, very different ways of being nuns. For instance, the Poor Clare takes a vow of radical poverty in imitation of Saint Francis, which is not a Benedictine vow. By contrast, a Benedictine's approach to poverty is implied through her vow of fidelity to the Benedictine life. Her approach is also based more around simplicity and a limitation of personal possessions than the stark poverty of Francis's poor ladies. Is one approach inherently better than the other? Absolutely not! Is only one charism a fool-proof method of salvation? Of course not. God calls certain women to follow one charism, and He calls others to a different one.

This is not to say that all ways of being a nun or a mom are equally good, nor is one valid charism equally suited for everyone. There are wonderful Carmelites who would wilt as Cistercians, and vice versa, just as there are flourishing mothers who would crash and burn if they tried a parenting style that didn't suit them. And then, unfortunately, there are both nuns and moms whose particular ways of living out their respective vocations are, simply put, mediocre. Oftentimes, this type of failure results from not being faithful or consistent to the realistic demands of our vocations.

Part of what attracts a woman to a particular monastic charism is her personality, her personal struggles, talents, and gifts. This is also true in regard to moms' go-to choices for parenting styles. Some women, sensing a deep need for order in their lives and the lives of their children, opt to parent in a way that emphasizes that; while others are drawn to styles that emphasize community, creativity, or independence.

Part of the angst surrounding parenting styles is a worry about finding the "right way" to parent, as if then we will have the user-manual for our children. Perhaps if we spent more time reflecting upon our chosen parenting approach as one motherly charism among several, dedicated to the end goal of holiness and human flourishing, we would find more peace both with our own choices and with the different paths taken by our fellow mothers.

Question

Moms compare themselves to other moms all the time. It is almost impossible not to, since there are so many ways to go about being a mother. I think we often start comparing ourselves because we are insecure about how we are doing as a mom, and we end by judging others or feeling judged by the moms around us—often harshly—for not managing to reach the ideal. How do we avoid judging and comparing those who are working out their vocations alongside us?

Answer by Mother Marija,
Byzantine Carmelites

Moms do this all the time—compare themselves to each other—and it is not healthy. God has the recipe, remember? He made you just the way you are, though yes, you are fallen and a sinner. But look at what He is sending you each day. Do not look at others. Look at what He sends each day and accept it. Really, we over-use our heads. That's the problem. The mind is the problem. The devil has a great mind. And it is the mind that distracts us from the heart. While we are worrying about what is in our minds, we are not making acts of gratitude for what is right before us. Our memory is a great gift, but our memory can lead us all over the place, which is not necessarily helpful or good! And so, the thing we must do is to try to pray, and to pray always, as Our Lord said—and He was not just thinking about religious when He said that!

A mistake that young people can fall into when they think about their vocations is this. If you've made something of a mess in your life—and some have—you might look upon marriage or the convent as a new beginning: "ok, I made a mess there, but now I am starting my vocation and can start life all over again. It is going to be a success." No! What the past was, you take with you. You cannot disown your past. That would be so reckless. But it would also be unfair to the people in your past and to your family. And very unfair to God.

So, there must be a great deal of acceptance; acceptance of whatever the Lord—and you—have done before you began your vocation. None of that is to be disowned as nonexistent. Of course, there may be areas where you need to have repentance, but then, for the love of God, stop focusing on that and remember that there is some hope! Otherwise, you will keep beating yourself up for too long a time.

And this is true for our approach to others as well. You cannot ask other people for a self-revelation or a self-reflection. The person might not even be able to do it! But watch and listen. What do you hear? It will come out of their mouth if you wait and listen to them. You will not even have to ask them! You might just have to listen for a long time. That is one of the good advantages of a lot of the silence in the monastery! It gives you a chance to listen to other people and see what you can learn about them. They do not have to tell you directly. Just listen.

Do not revisit the past. Thank God for what you did right and be thankful that things are as good as they are now. Unfortunately, too many people do visit the past. I am a very present person—no credit to me! I have a great memory for all the wrong things. There was a sister who was Polish and a real hardliner, which I liked. I liked her because she was always the same, always a hardliner. She was good. One day, she met up with me in the hall and said, "I've figured you out! Yes. You have an impractical memory! You remember people's names, addresses, phone numbers, but you cannot find your clothes or your shoes!" And she was right. I remember the Battle of Hastings—1066!—but do not ask me where my phone is! So, we must be who we are and take life as it is. We cannot do everything and be everything.

Today, we have God's grace. Yesterday, His mercy. Tomorrow, His providence. And so, we do not have to worry. God will get out of bed before us tomorrow. We do not have to worry because Jesus is full of mercy, and because today, we have the Holy Spirit and the Grace of Christ. All we must do is simply work on today—not our past and its shortcomings.

Question

Different monastic orders have different charisms. There is also a vast difference in ways women respond to the call to be physical mothers. We have so many different styles, emphases, and approaches. I know that a lot of moms judge each other based on different parenting styles. Obviously, sometimes there are better and worse ways to be a mom, just like there can be better and worse ways of being a monastic. However, I wonder if it would be useful for moms to think of our chosen approaches to parenting more along the lines of charism, like monastics have, rather than in our often judgmental reactions to each others' different methods. Isn't it true that charisms emphasize different ways of doing the same thing—being a monastic—in a way that doesn't exclude other established charisms as valid alternatives? Could you please help me understand how charism works?

Answer by Mother Abbess Cecilia, Benedictines

Every religious order has a different method of following Christ. He left behind a very beautiful visible life that has integral components but can receive emphasis in a multitude of ways. Poverty, chastity, and obedience are common to almost all religious, but the way of life is vastly different from order to order. The more faithful we are to the way of life, the happier we are.

There is a lot of variety: Passionists keep something of a daily Good Friday, whereas Redemptorists have a monthly Christmas, which they call "Little Christmas." Carmelites emulate Christ in solitude, communing with His Father, while we Benedictines idealize the warmth of Nazareth, praying and working as a family. We feel strongest together and so draw strength from the liturgy. Everyone else is bound to the liturgy, but we "do it up" more, kind of like a musical family.

We see this in families too; everyone has their "thing." Some are musical, as I mentioned, some are outdoorsy types, others are intellectuals, others do a lot of sports together. Some place great emphasis on the meal together, others just want to play board games in the living room. But the principle guiding each family is striving for holiness within their dynamic and among the people and circumstances with whom God has placed them. Unlike a religious community, where the spirituality is set, each family forms their own charism. Now, this leaves a very wide berth. But even so, it can be beautiful, especially if unity is sought.

Even in a religious community, where we are all following the same rule, there is a particular interpretation upon which we all agree. When associating with one another, or even other communities, there must be a great latitude as well. Every soul is called to holiness in the context of her community and particular family, admitting there will always be differences of opinion in minor matters that do not threaten our salvation. Our sanctification is passing into God's own life, His intended vision for us, and that is going to vary between persons, just as there is variance among flowers. Accepting differences leads us forward in great peace.

So too with the particular charism in each house. You can have the same order manifesting the charism differently, just like the different generations of the same family. Some traditions are kept, others are discontinued. Respect and trust are shown to the forthcoming generations, just like in an ordered home in which adult children are trusted to make good decisions. There was a mother who, when complimented about her grown children, was asked her secret. "Do your best, and then get out of the way."

In foundations, we strive to be the same way, trusting each house with the application of prayer for priests and house customs. Hospitality is emphasized at our Abbey, for example, but less so at our daughter house, owing to their remote location. Here, we see that God has placed them in circumstances that point to a more prayerful support of the Diocese rather than welcoming priests for retreat from across the country.

The Litany of the Holy Spirit

Lord, have mercy on us.

Christ, have mercy on us.

Lord, have mercy on us.

Father all powerful,

Have mercy on us.

Jesus, Eternal Son of the Father,
    Redeemer of the world, save us.

Spirit of the Father and the Son, boundless
    Life of both, sanctify us.

Holy Trinity, hear us.

Holy Spirit, Who proceeds from the Father
    and the Son, enter our hearts.

Holy Spirit, Who art equal to the Father
    and the Son, enter our hearts.

Promise of God the Father, have mercy on us.

Ray of heavenly light, have mercy on us.

Author of all good, etc.

Source of Heavenly water,

Consuming Fire,

Ardent Charity,

Spiritual Unction,

Spirit of love and truth,

Spirit of wisdom and understanding,

Spirit of counsel and fortitude,

Spirit of knowledge and piety,

Spirit of the fear of the Lord,

Spirit of grace and prayer,

Spirit of peace and meekness,

Spirit of modesty and innocence,

Holy Spirit, the Comforter,

Holy Spirit, the Sanctifier,

Holy Spirit, Who governs the Church,

Gift of God the Most High,

Spirit Who fillest the universe,

Spirit of the adoption of the children of God,

Holy Spirit, inspire us with horror of sin.

Holy Spirit, come and renew the face of the earth.

Holy Spirit, shed Thy light into our souls.

Holy Spirit, engrave Thy law in our hearts.

Holy Spirit, inflame us with the flame of Thy love.

Holy Spirit, open to us the treasures of Thy graces.

Holy Spirit, teach us to pray well.

Holy Spirit, enlighten us with Thy
Heavenly inspirations.

Holy Spirit, lead us in the way of salvation.

Holy Spirit, grant us the only necessary knowledge.

Holy Spirit, inspire in us the practice of good.

Holy Spirit, grant us the merits of all virtues.

Holy Spirit, make us persevere injustice.

Holy Spirit, be our everlasting reward.

Lamb of God, Who takest away the sins of the world,
Send us Thy Holy Spirit.

Lamb of God, Who takest away the sins of the world,
Pour down into our souls the gifts of the Holy Spirit.

Lamb of God, Who takest away the sins of the world,
Grant us the Spirit of wisdom and piety.

V. Come, Holy Spirit! Fill the hearts of Thy faithful,

R. And enkindle in them the fire of Thy love.

Let Us Pray.

Grant, O merciful Father, that Thy Divine Spirit may enlighten, inflame and purify us, that He may penetrate us with His heavenly dew and make us fruitful in good works, through Our Lord Jesus Christ, Thy Son, Who with Thee, in the unity of the same Spirit, liveth and reigneth forever and ever.

R. Amen.

CHAPTER 9

Silence

"Silence is necessary, and even absolutely necessary.
If silence is lacking, then grace is lacking."

—Saint Maximilian Kolbe

Ah, silence. If silence were truly golden, mothers would be beggars and nuns would be millionaires! Silence is a key feature of monastic life—the Carthusians, for instance, barring monastic chant during prayers, only engage in a few minutes' worth of conversation once a week. Most other contemplatives are a bit chattier than that and—contrary to a popular myth—no order takes an actual vow of silence. They live quietly throughout the day, speaking only when necessary, except during times that are set apart for socialization. Occasionally, Carmelites spend time in special hermitages on the monastic grounds to be more silent and focused. In the Middle Ages, the Cistercians and Benedictines invented a form of sign language so that even their essential communications could be done silently—and there are a few monasteries today that still practice it. Silence has earned the name of the "mother tongue" of monastics by writer George Prochnik in his book, *In Pursuit of Silence.*

As for us moms, well, if your house is anything like mine, I do not even get the privacy of the bathroom to collect my thoughts! The other day, I spent my shower time answering questions bellowed through the door because there was a burning need to know a random fact about beetles versus spiders that just could not wait! The radio in the car goes unused because at any given moment, there are three songs in different genres and in various degrees of key coming from the back seat. And in the silent moments of Mass, I am mostly occupied with keeping the noise levels down in our pew. Silence and I are barely acquaintances, much less friends.

Many people, myself included, do not really know what to do with silence when we find it. Partly, this is because it is nigh impossible to achieve silence for long. Even when our children are quiet or we find ourselves alone, the modern world has been designed in such a way that noise is everywhere. You do not need me to rehash the universally acknowledged reality that modern people seem to fear silence: we have YouTube, iTunes, Audible, and podcasts to fill up the air, and televisions, tablets, and smartphones everywhere to catch and hold our attention. If all of that were suddenly taken away and we found ourselves in the quiet, many of us would immediately become fidgety and uncomfortable. According to one rather horrible study from a few years ago, many people would rather receive electric shocks than be left alone with their quiet thoughts for just a few minutes.[71]

Therefore, for most of us, silence is both a luxury we crave and an unwelcome stranger that we fear. In that way, it is like most things that are good for us: hard to get and difficult to appreciate until we have made it a discipline. But monastics are not the only ones who need silence. In fact, you can think of silence as a form of spiritual homemaking. Cultivating moments of silence nurtures us as persons.

Thomas Merton, or Brother Lewis, as he was known to his fellow Trappists, explains best what I mean by this:

> Not all men are called to be hermits, but all men need enough silence and solitude in their lives to enable the deep inner voice of their own true self to be heard at least occasionally. When that inner voice is not heard, when man cannot attain to the spiritual peace that comes from being perfectly at one with his true self, his life is always miserable and exhausting. For he cannot go on happily for long unless he is in contact with the springs of spiritual life which are hidden in the depths of his own soul. If man is constantly exiled from his own home, locked out of his

[71] Timothy D. Wilson, et al. "Just think: The challenges of the disengaged mind," Science, 345, 6192 (2014), 75–77.DOI:10.1126 /science.1250830.

own spiritual solitude, he ceases to be a true person. He no longer lives as a man.[72]

In this silence and solitude of the inner recesses of our soul's home, our soul encounters the quiet voice of God in His secret whispers to our inmost self. Even us moms who are surrounded by the busy babble of home life need moments of this silence and quiet for our spiritual health. Perhaps the secret lies not so much in replicating the copious amounts of silence available in religious life, but in learning how best to use what silence we can find.

Question

I often find that when I encounter silence—especially in church or in time set aside for quiet prayer—I cannot shut myself up! There is too much to worry about, plan for, or to consider that it ends up crowding its way into my mind when I am seeking silence and reflection. How can we silence that inner crowd when we turn to pray?

Answer by Mother Mary Angela and the Roswell Poor Clares

First of all, the challenge of silencing the "inner crowd" is definitely experienced by Poor Clares! The sisters had many practical suggestions to share.

---

[72]   Thomas Merton, *The Silent Life* (New York: Farrar, Straus & Giroux, 1957), 166–167.

To help with the things to plan or which you need to worry about: making a list of what has to be done (outside of prayer time) is helpful, so that there is not the anxiety of whether we will remember what we have to do next! Also, writing out what is troubling us can be helpful—just to get it out on paper—and share it with Our Lord! (I think this can be done during prayer time, as a kind of journaling, although we try to keep this kind of practice brief.)

About distractions: when a distraction is standing in front of you, try "looking over its shoulder" to focus on prayer. Or make a prayer out of the very distraction! If worry is occupying you, take it to God and speak with Him about it. Saint Teresa of Ávila referred to the imagination as the madwoman of the house. Her writing is very helpful on this subject (and on so many others pertaining to prayer).

At the beginning of prayer time, take a moment to just quiet down in prayer, ask the Holy Spirit to help you focus and be attentive. It can be helpful to have a text from Scripture or some other spiritual reading to help you be attentive. Make the choice, the deliberate choice, to pray, and to be happy and grateful to be there, and to have the time to pray; to say to Our Lord, "I want to be here right now, and I am glad to be here. There is nowhere else in the world I would rather be." It helps to remember that if we are seeking God, He is seeking us first; we want to be content to be with Him who is so content to be with us.

Keeping our prayer very simple is also helpful; not to try for complicated prayer. Saint Bernadette said that when you feel as if you cannot pray, that is the time to pray to Saint Joseph.

Father Jeremiah Shryock CFR says that "prayer is looking at Jesus." Repeating the Holy Names of Jesus and Mary to become recollected. Sometimes a short prayer or chant or invocation, such as "Jesus, I trust in You!", can be very helpful in settling down to pray. Just opening the Scriptures and allowing God to speak can be very grace-filled.

We have our own ideas about what makes our prayer good; it may be pleasing to God when we have struggled and been distracted the whole time! He sees our effort, our struggles, our desires.

If possible, rising early (before the family) can provide a good time to pray in silence. Also, try to have a little place in the home where the family members can pray, some kind of little altar.

Many years ago, Mother Mary Francis was speaking to a priest about her prayer life. She felt very "pulled in all directions" and was concerned that sometimes she was not able to take as much time in prayer as she would have liked. The priest told her, "Mother, the Sisters are your prayer." So perhaps we can apply this to say for mothers, "Your children are your prayer." The Church Father Tertullian's own father knelt before his son's cradle to adore the Blessed Trinity in his son's heart and soul.

Finally, unite yourself with Our Lady, and as you perform the same duties that she once did, think of how you are meeting the same needs that she did (as when nursing the baby).

Question

Perhaps the most obvious difference that a mom and a nun have in our daily lives is the noise level! My house is barely ever quiet, while your monastery probably goes weeks without a truly loud crash, bang, or shout. I know when my fellow moms and I talk about nuns, we envy the quiet. It seems like it would be so easy to pray! This might seem like an odd question, but I want to know what is the best use of silence? If I can only manage a few moments of silence in a day, how can I best use it spiritually?

Answer by Sister Anne Marie, Cistercians of the Valley of Our Lady

With the gift of faith, you know by faith that Jesus lives in you. He tells us, abide in Me as I abide in you.[73] As best you can, give Him your attention in those few moments. Turn to Him in faith and allow Him to look at you. Jesus said to Nathaniel, "Before Philip called you . . . I saw you."[74] That is how it really is! He sees you. You are caring

---

[73] See Jn 15:4.
[74] Jn 1:48.

for His children with the love of your motherly heart. The look on His face and in His eyes is one of gratitude and joy that His children are being loved and cared for by you. He sees you and watches over you, and maybe He sees His own mother in you.

Now, let me correct a misunderstanding. The silence that fills our days and nights in a monastery is not some "magic" that makes prayer easy and perfect. We spend our entire lives trying to pray, desiring to pray, and all this with the experience of, day in and day out, praying so poorly. This is God's great school for teaching us to grow in trust of Him and His love through *acceptance* of our poverty. We slowly learn that God responds most fully to prayer of the heart poured out from our emptiness and poverty . . . and poured out from your motherly heart in the midst of all the sounds (not noise!) that fill a home where children are growing up.

Answer by Sister Christina, Capuchin Sisters of Nazareth

It is no secret that we have been robbed of silence by a culture of constant noise and distraction. Yet, even in a noisy home with children, inner silence is possible. Silence doesn't necessarily mean the absence of noise, but a "silent heart" that is open to hearing God's voice in the commonplace of the crying two-year-old, the dinner table, and the pile of laundry.

If you're graced as a mother with a moment of silence, perhaps you'll find the following steps helpful:

1. Offer a prayer of praise. Praise is a powerful form of prayer and perhaps the most neglected. Praise looks at God, not at self. We praise God simply because He *is* God, because He is worthy of praise. No other prayer can free us so beautifully from the thousand cares, worries, and responsibilities of our daily lives.

2. Let go of distractions. As you offer your prayer of praise, it's likely you'll hear the distractions creep in. Let them go, if only for a moment. Jesus said to Josefa Menéndez, "Do I not know that family cares, household concerns, and the requirements of your position in life make continual calls upon you? Cannot you spare a few minutes in which to come and prove your affection and your gratitude?"[75]

3. Adore the Holy Spirit within you. Keep in mind that you don't have to be in a church to be with God. While nothing can replace His Sacramental Presence, you can make within your heart a little chapel, where the Holy Spirit is present. A simple act of adoration, however brief, is most pleasing to God.

[75] Sr. Josefa Menedez, "The Blessed Sacrament and Sinners: March 1st-11th, 1923." In *The Way of Divine Love*. Sands, London, 1950. https://www.ecatholic2000.com/way/untitled-50.shtml#_Toc380718970.

Psalm 62, a Hymn of King David

For God alone my soul waits in silence;
   from him comes my salvation.

He only is my rock and my salvation,
   my fortress; I shall not be greatly moved.

How long will you set upon a man
   to shatter him, all of you,
   like a leaning wall, a tottering fence?

They only plan to thrust him down
   from his eminence.

They take pleasure in falsehood.

They bless with their mouths,
   but inwardly they curse.   *Selah*

For God alone my soul waits in silence,
   for my hope is from him.

He only is my rock and my salvation,
   my fortress; I shall not be shaken.

On God rests my deliverance and my honor;
   my mighty rock, my refuge is God.

Trust in him at all times, O people;
   pour out your heart before him;

God is a refuge for us.   *Selah*

Men of low estate are but a breath,
   men of high estate are a delusion;

in the balances they go up;
   they are together lighter than a breath.

Put no confidence in extortion,
  set no vain hopes on robbery;
  if riches increase, set not your heart on them.

Once God has spoken;
  twice have I heard this:

that power belongs to God;
  and that to thee, O Lord, belongs steadfast love.

For thou dost requite a man
  according to his work.

CHAPTER 10

Poverty

On January 16, 1933, while looking out of her kitchen window, twelve-year-old Mariette Beco saw a young woman dressed all in white with a veil and blue sash standing in the garden, smiling and beckoning to her. Her mother, who saw nobody, forbade her to go outside. But over the course of the next two months, Mariette saw the woman again and again. The lady called herself "Our Lady of the Poor."[76]

This little-known apparition at Banneux, Belgium, in the poverty-stricken years between the two World Wars, is beautifully similar to the much more famous apparitions at Lourdes; so much so that the visionary's disbelieving aunt mockingly referred to her as "Bernadette," before the local bishop became convinced of the veracity of Mariette's claims and referred the matter to Rome. Our Lady even gave the little village a miraculous healing stream that, even to this day, draws pilgrims seeking cures.

---

[76] The apparitions (1933). Banneux Notre-Dame. https://banneux -nd.be/en/the-apparitions/.

Like Saint Bernadette, Mariette viewed herself as simply a humble tool in the hands of the Queen of Heaven. Bernadette compared herself to a broom: "The Virgin used me as a broom to remove the dust. When the work is done, the broom is put behind the door again."[77] For her part, Mariette said, "I was no more than a postman who delivers the mail. Once this has been done, the postman is of no importance any more."[78] Bernadette retired to a convent to pursue her vocation; Mariette quietly married and raised a family.

The most striking thing about the apparitions at Banneux is Our Lady's chosen title: Our Lady of the Poor. 1930s Belgium was caught in a brutal economic depression that would only be made worse with the second World War. During this economic hardship, Our Lady wanted to remind us that, although she is the Queen of Heaven, she is also one of the poor.

Poverty was not simply a burden that Mary and Joseph accepted in their earthly lives, but it was something they embraced. In fact, one of Saint Joseph's titles is "Lover of Poverty." Such a title does not mean that he is simply the

---

[77]   "February 11: Our Lady of Lourdes—Optional Memorial." My Catholic Life! https://mycatholic.life/saints/saints-of-the-liturgical-year/february-11-our-lady-of-lourdes/#:~:text=Several%20years%20after%20her%20visions,was%20much%20bigger%20than%20Bernadette.

[78]   Madeleine Teahan, "Visionary who reported eight apparitions of Mary dies aged 90." Catholic Herald.co.uk. December 7, 2011. https://web.archive.org/web/20131212215754/http://www.catholicherald.co.uk/news/2011/12/07/visionary-who-reported-eight-apparitions-of-mary-dies-aged-90/.

benefactor of poor people, but that there is something about poverty itself that he loves.

Similarly, in the first Marian hymn, the Magnificat, in which Mary sang out her joy at having been chosen to be the Mother of God, she notes specifically that God has respected her lowliness—loved her because of her little-ness and poverty. She still cherishes her connection to the poor because of the hidden value she knows poverty can contain for those who embrace it.

Mother Mary Francis, in her wonderful book, *Strange Gods Before Me*, describes a scene of Poor Clares delight-ing in the glory and joy that is attached to their radical poverty. It is the abbess's fiftieth anniversary as a pro-fessed nun, and her monastic daughters are decorating the refectory to celebrate. Poor Clares do not go out and buy supplies—they await the charity of others and make do with what they have. In this scene, Mother Mary Francis describes the nuns bringing out a gold-rimmed saucer, which had its origins in a Quaker Oats box, and festooning their abbess's humble chair with an old silk parachute. She comments gleefully that you cannot imag-ine how many uses Poor Clares have for that parachute.[79]

I was struck by just how *fun* poverty seems to Mother Mary Francis. If they had gone out and purchased party supplies, would it have been quite as enjoyable? It reminded me of my own children, who, also not able to

---

[79]   Mother Mary Francis, P.C.C., *Strange Gods Before Me* (Poor Clares: 2020), 14–15.

simply purchase whatever they may want, have a thousand uses for the little random odds and ends they have accumulated. There are some marbles tucked away in a little wooden box more precious to their young owners than my best earrings are to me. Mother Mary Francis describes a childlike embrace of poverty that turns odds and ends into riches in the name of fun, joy, and, most importantly, love.

Embracing poverty is a staple of religious life, even in monastic orders that do not have a specific vow of poverty. Most famously, we have Saint Francis of Assisi, God's poor man, who embraced radical poverty to such an extent that he enjoined those in his order to beg for their bread, wear the roughest garments, and even go without shoes. While it is a natural human instinct to fear poverty, Saint Francis proclaims that "poverty is that heavenly virtue by which all earthy and transitory things are trodden under foot, and by which every obstacle is removed from the soul so that it may freely enter into union with the eternal Lord God."[80]

But this same acceptance of poverty—even seeking it as a Christian virtue—is a struggle for many parents. It is often difficult to remember the spiritual potential in poverty, rightly practiced, in a world that looks down its nose at most forms of self-denial. Motherhood is full of its share of poverty, though it does not always look the same for each of us. Raising children is a financial

[80] Brother Ugolino, *Little Flowers of Saint Francis of Assisi*. William Heywood, Translator (Cosimo Classics: 2007), 35.

burden, and parents are called upon to sacrifice comfort, time, hobbies, and careers for the sake of their families. This is especially true of large families and families with a stay-at-home mother in a society that increasingly is not designed for such family dynamics.

Then there is the poverty that is less financial so much as it is one of lifestyle. I remember being a teenager wondering why my parents liked dented furniture . . . oblivious to the fact that my siblings and I were the cause of it! As a parent myself, I have had plenty of opportunities to repent of my childhood disregard for my parents' possessions! There is a poverty of spirit in charitably embracing the dishes broken by unpracticed, childish hands.

Saint Augustine of Hippo hints at this spiritual power of poverty when he says,

> God means to fill each of you with what is good; so cast out what is bad! If he wishes to fill you with honey and you are full of sour wine, where is the honey to go? The vessel must be emptied of its contents and then be cleansed. Yes, it must be cleansed even if you have to work hard and scour it. It must be made fit for the new thing, whatever it may be. We may go on speaking figuratively of honey, gold or wine—but whatever we say we cannot express the reality we are to receive. The name of that reality is God.[81]

---

[81] Augustine of Hippo, "Augustine of Hippo: God Enlarges the Capacity of Our Soul that He may Fill Us with His Presence." Enlarging the Heart, February 18, 2011. Taken from "Homilies on the First

How do we, as mothers, allow ourselves to be emptied, so that we may be filled?

Question

There's that old cliché expression, "this is why we can't have nice things." A mom friend of mine won't have people over because she is embarrassed about the state of her furniture—her kids are a bit tough on couches, chairs, and tables. Of course, I cannot say I'm much better. I spent a whole afternoon silently furious because of innocent, childish scuff marks and handprints on a freshly painted wall. I suppose part of being a mom is accepting and offering as a sacrifice the reality that our kids often will make our homes look very lived-in. Maybe this is a mom's vow of poverty, in a way of speaking, because it asks her to forego material goods for the sake of her children's well-being. How can we embrace poverty, and what are the benefits of poverty?

Answer by Mother Mary Angela and the Roswell Poor Clares

In religious life, poverty is practiced by taking care of things; not necessarily expensive things but taking care of what we are given to use. Poverty is not about

Letter of St John, Hom. 4," found in the Office of Readings for Friday of the 6th week in Ordinary Time. Crossroads Initiative. https ://enlargingtheheart.wordpress.com/2011/02/18/augustine-of -hippo-god-enlarges-the-capacity-of-our-soul-that-he-may-fill-us -with-his-presence/.

run-down things, but about care of things. Because those who live in poverty do not have a lot in terms of materiality, they (hopefully) learn to care for what they do have.

One sister shared her still-vivid memory of a spanking received as a child, and richly deserved, for leaving an expensive book outdoors and for the book being damaged by an accidental sprinkling from a garden hose! It taught her a lasting lesson about responsibility for valuable items. Other sisters remembered being trained not to damage things, but to respect and care for them. The child needs discipline, to be told how to care for things—explanation is important.

Having child-friendly furniture is also very helpful—trying to raise children in a house with valuable antiques would seem rather foolish! There is always a balance—allowing children to play and romp without becoming destructive, to have toys but not to leave them littered all over the house, etc.

About the benefits of poverty—it brings lightness of heart and lifts our minds to "things above." There is a great benefit to learning to live simply, without a lot of extras, without things that are not really necessary. There can be so much pressure on people to have things that are not really needed, simply because "everyone else has one."

Another benefit of poverty is ingenuity; when one can learn to make do with what one has, or find ways to supply needs, including inventions!

Question

For many parents and would-be parents, the cost of raising a child is rather intimidating. Plus, I know that many people struggle with the idea of having a larger family because of financial concerns. Obviously, God does not ask us to be financially irresponsible when it comes to our families. But still, it is often hard to willingly embrace the financial limitations that go along with the call to be fruitful and multiply. There are so many worldly goods that seem important and that can, at times, challenge us as we seek to live out our vocations. Please share some thoughts about your own experience with poverty as part of your vocation.

Answer by Mother Marija,
Byzantine Carmelites

When I decided to try to found this monastery, my old monastery was glad to see me go. I was not going to do the secular clothes, the communion services with Anglicans, and all that, so I decided I was going to try to start this monastery. But what did I have? There were four of us sisters with one thousand dollars among us. We had a car, but we had no food. We had the habits on our backs, some books, and that was it. We came out here to where the monastery is now and realized nobody had thought of supper. The monastery was just an old farmhouse that was a home for woodchucks! To add to that, I had no money, we did not know anybody, and there was nobody to ask for help!

That night, one of the sisters found some big cans somewhere. I don't know what we ate, but we did eat something. And then I took a statue of Saint Joseph that I had taken from my old Carmel and said, "we will pray to Saint Joseph." Of course, that is what I had asked to take with me from the old place—statues and stuff—not anything sensible! I prayed to Saint Joseph to send us friends and food, and we still pray that novena every single day.

We had just finished the novena that night when there was a knock on the door. . . The bishop was there at the door! Turns out he had been visiting the Franciscans down the road. He said, "I have come to be your friend. Here is something for food." He then gave me a hundred dollars. I had just prayed for friends and food—and here they were.

I can only say that, in my seventy-eight years of Carmelite life, there have been many days that were difficult, but I never, never regretted entering. I was never truly unhappy. Suffering is not the same as being unhappy. When you are suffering, you are suffering; you aren't jolly, but you can take it. You can live with it.

And so that is all I can say. Somehow, we ended up here, in this monastery, sitting here today on a couch that some man donated in 1980. We just kept going.

Question

Every time I step on a Lego brick late at night in my kids'
playroom or sit down to fold laundry, I get the urge to
throw most of our possessions away! I remember being
a poor graduate student, able to fit all my worldly goods
into a couple of duffle bags. There was something rather
liberating about that lack of stuff. Now, as a mom of many
children surrounded by piles of clothes, toys, books, and
chaos, I sometimes miss the simplicity of owning barely
anything. The thing is, I know that my kids do need things,
and quite a lot of things, in our home. Still, I struggle to
know how to strike a balance between my competing desire
to make sure my kids have a comfortable home and the
desire for simplicity. How do you strike a balance between
material needs and a desire for austerity?

Answer by Sister Anne Marie,
Cistercians of the Valley of Our Lady

We want to be careful to give ourselves the "freedom" to
make our own decisions about what real "needs" are. Our
culture places exaggerated emphasis on material things
and wants to convince us that our "happiness" comes
from having this, that, and the next thing. Such a cul-
tural mind-set can subtly work on all of us, especially on
mothers and fathers who are trying to lead their children
in a way of self-restraint and discipline in regard to feeling that they need a lot of things.

Parents can have pressure put on them so they begin
to "feel" they are not being generous with their children

if they don't give them all the newest toys the friends of their children may have. For children growing up with the *gift* of family life, having siblings to play with is way beyond the gift of toys. Certainly, children can have some toys, but a few good toys for the various age groups is probably about all that is needed. If it seems too many toys have accumulated, it might be time to give the children the experience of real joy that can come from a sacrifice of giving a favorite toy to a poor child. It might be difficult to "find" poor children. But a big part of the "joy" of the sacrifice can come when they actually hand over their toy in person to another child. Maybe the parish secretary would know of a poor family.

Another aspect of material things has to do with clothes. Clothes are needed and raising a family with all the members needing clothes can make the pile of laundry a rather daunting task (at least on some days). Doing the laundry is just one more motherly service of love. Older children can be great helpers with the laundry. As a way of teaching the children a good Christian detachment, help them see that they don't need to have all the latest fashions. They may think they need something because "everyone else has it." This kind of "following the crowd" can lead later to older children making less-than-good decisions. Of course, children want to feel accepted by their peers, but good guidance and help early in their life can be very formative in giving them the freedom they need to be themselves.

Prayer of Bishop Louis-Joseph Kerkhofs, Bishop of Liège, during the apparitions of Our Lady at Banneux

O Virgin of the Poor,

May you ever be blessed!

And blessed be He who deigned to send you to us.

What you have been and are to us now,

you will always be to those who, like
us, and better than us,

offer their faith and their prayer.

You will be all for us, as you revealed
yourself at Banneux:

Mediatrix of all graces, the Mother of
the Savior, Mother of God.

A compassionate and powerful Mother
who loves the poor and all People,

who alleviates suffering, who saves
individuals and all humanity,

Queen and Mother of all Nations,

who came to lead all those who allow
themselves to be guided by you,

to Jesus the true and only Source of eternal life.

Amen.

CHAPTER 11

Balancing Work and Prayer

"If you don't pray, your presence will have no power,
your words will have no power. If you pray, you will
be able to overcome all the tricks of the devil."

—Saint Mother Teresa of Calcutta

I once saw an altered version of Saint Benedict's *ora et labora*, "pray and work:" it read, *laborare est orare*, "work is prayer." That is, of course, true on a certain level. Saint Thérèse of Liseux, in her *Little Way*, reminds us that something as simple as picking up a pin for the glory of God is a magnificent form of prayer. And Saint Paul admonishes us in Philippians 2:12 that we are to "work out [our] salvation." *Laborare est orare*, for any good work done in love for God and our neighbor is a form of prayer.

But Saint Thérèse did not spend her entire life simply picking up pins, and Saint Paul also entreats us, in 1 Timothy 2:1–2, to pray hard: "I urge that supplications, prayers, intercessions, and thanksgivings be made for all men, for kings and all who are in high positions, that we may lead a quiet and peaceable life, godly and respectful in every way." While work can be a form of prayer, it is important to remember that it is not the only or the best form of prayer. Saint Benedict separated the two for a reason in his famous dictum.

There is something more sacred and significant in prayer that pauses from all work and focuses the created soul directly upon its creator. Martha was hardly choosing poorly when she prepared food for her Lord and his apostles, but it was still Mary who chose the better part in her silent sitting and listening at His feet.

But how are we to strike a balance? This is quite difficult, not simply for mothers, but for the world at large. There are just so many pressing issues to attend to that we often feel guilty about surrendering to the call of prayer that is not also work. This is exacerbated by the modern world's incessant demand for *action* in politics, culture, and even the Church. The modern world is frenzied in its focus on doing something that yields immediate, tangible results. If I can praise God by means of clothing the naked and feeding the hungry, do I have any right to pause in that vital mission to just praise God alone?

Contemplation is foreign to the result-driven world of today because it does not understand what it is. Saint Teresa of Ávila explains, "contemplative prayer, in my opinion, is nothing else than a close sharing between friends; it means taking time frequently to be alone with Him who we know loves us."[82]

Saint Teresa of Calcutta, a saint known primarily through her tireless good works, has this to say about prayer: "If we neglect prayer and if the branch is not connected with the vine, it will die. That connecting of branch with vine is prayer. If that connection is there then love is there, then joy is there, and we will be the sunshine of God's love, the hope of eternal happiness, the flame of burning love. Why? Because we are one with Jesus."[83] And how did Mother Teresa pray? Not simply through her work, or during her work, but in a time and space set apart. Agreeing with Saint Teresa of Ávila, Mother Teresa sought stillness in contemplative prayer: "For the more we receive in silent prayer, the more we can give in our active life. We need silence to be able to touch souls. The essential thing is not what we say, but what God says to us."[84]

Mothers should not simply serve our children by doing chores and tasks for them—we should serve them with our presence and our undivided attention, loving them by sharing ourselves with them. We must *be,* and not only *do.* Just so, we should also serve our God with

---

[82] Teresa of Jesus, *The Book of Her Life,* 8,5 in *The Collected Works of St. Teresa of Avila.* K. Kavanagh, and O. Rodriguez, translators. (Washington DC: Institute of Carmelite Studies, 1976), 1, 67.

[83] Angelo Devananda, *Mother Teresa: Contemplative at the Heart of the World.* (Collins, Fount Paperbacks, 1985), 102.

[84] Angelo Devananda, *Mother Teresa,* 100.

our presence, not forcing Him into the corners of the day, giving him only the remnants of our attention, even if the dishes are not all the way done, or the laundry is not quite folded or the math not quite graded. After all, if we wish to show our love, should we not prioritize the beloved?

Question

It is so easy to get discouraged in prayer. There are so many chores that stack up around the house and so many needs from the members of my household that demand my attention. I often find myself shoving prayer into tiny corners of the day, and even prioritizing other things to the point where I end up in bed having not set aside any time at all to pray. I tell myself I'll pray while working, but often, that doesn't happen. Still, setting aside time to pray is often stressful—another item on the long list of things I hope to cram into the day. How can I make sure that prayer does not end up being "just another item on the checklist"?

Answer by Mother Mary Angela and the Roswell Poor Clares

Here are some practical suggestions:

Praying as a family, especially, when the children are old enough, praying the Rosary together. One sister remembered their family of four children doing this with their parents throughout their childhood years. When Mom was not well, they would kneel around her bed, but they always prayed the Rosary together. Another way to pray as a family is praying grace before and after meals. The children learn discipline, and that the family is supposed to pray every day.

For personal prayer time, it was suggested to try to take it as early as possible in the day, scheduling it in. Probably not long spaces of time, but some time just for Him. God doesn't need long stretches of time to work in our hearts.

Praying throughout the day with simple aspirations, invocations, or offering daily chores as a prayer: "All for love of you, O Jesus;" "Getting into 'conversation mode' with Jesus."

Not having television can be immensely helpful—there is time to do things together and to pray, not to mention the distractions that are avoided.

"Lock yourself in the bathroom for a couple of minutes!" Saint Ambrose says, "Every place is a place of prayer, though our Savior says, 'Go into your room' not a room enclosed by walls . . . but the room that is within you, the place where you hide your thoughts, where you keep your affections. This room of prayer is always with you, wherever you are, and it is always a secret room where only God can see you."[85]

---

[85] Saint Ambrose of Milan. Excerpt from Treatise on Cain and Abel, as included in the Liturgy of the Hours, Monday of the 27th week in Ordinary Time. https://divineoffice.org/ord-w27-mon-or/.

Question

What are the best and simplest ways to find, honor, and pray to Jesus in all the busyness of life?

Answer by Mother Marija, Byzantine Carmelites

You must find at least a little closet in your mind and in your heart. Put it in your heart, but your mind has to designate it. That is God's space that you can visit. It is not just your faith in God, but faith become prayer. That is important. And for mothers, that prayer does not have to be a set time and place. I would say it is an adjustable schedule for you, your schedule with God. He understands if it is down to ten seconds a day, but do try to at least show up for those ten seconds.

Saint Thérèse of Lisieux is an incredible example for a lot of people. Some context, so you know where I am coming from: at age thirteen, when I decided that I wanted to be a nun, I did not know where. I did not think the nuns who were teaching me were perfect enough—God forgive! So, I went into the library one day and asked the librarian sister for a biography of the great Saint Teresa of Ávila, because I had decided I should become a Carmelite, and I had better find out what they are like. But the library did not have a copy! Instead, the librarian handed me a biography of the Little Flower. Well, I said, "No thanks! No little flowers for me!" And I walked out! So, I never read Saint Thérèse until I got to Carmel. When I finally read her works, I thought, "Wow. I do not have what she has got. She loves God incredibly and I have got to figure out how to do this."

So, what do you do? You must move your prayer from your head to your heart and designate some time—maybe only five minutes a day or something. But you must do something and make yourself accountable to Him. You must also develop a relationship with Him, that is very important. He will respond. And, for your part, you must keep at it.

Remember the importance of receiving Holy Communion. Also, take one thing that you would like to give Him—some sacrifice—and make that a matter of examination of conscience. It does not have to be a big thing, or a lot, but it has to be constant, clear, and not too changeable. Then you have got to show up.

There is a story, and I don't know whether it's true, but the story is that there was this workman who used to go every day past the doors of Saint Peter's Church of Barclay Street. And he used to run into the door, kneel in the vestibule, and say, "Hi Jesus! It's Jimmy!" and then run on off to work. And one day, he was hurt on the job, and a priest brought him Extreme Unction, and when he saw the Host, he heard, "Hi Jimmy, it's Jesus." So, that little act was returned.

Prayer of Cardinal Newman

May the Lord support us all the day long,

Till the shades lengthen and the evening comes,

and the busy world is hushed, and
    the fever of life is over,

and our work is done.

Then in his mercy may he give us a safe lodging,

and holy rest, and peace at the last.

Amen.

CHAPTER 12

Prayer and Perfection

"Man is most wisely commanded to walk with right
steps, on purpose that, when he has discovered his own
inability to do even this, he may seek the remedy which is
provided for the inward man to cure the lameness of sin,
even the grace of God, through our Lord Jesus Christ."

—Saint Augustine of Hippo

Question: How do you know there is a Holy Day of
Obligation this week?
Answer: my husband is on a business trip.

Ok, it is not absolutely true, but it happens more often
than you would believe. It would be funny at this point
if it was not so stressful. Once, the Feast of the Immaculate Conception was not spent meditating upon this
glorious feast of our great heavenly mother, but stress-
ing about how to handle a nursing baby, two toddlers,
and a six-year-old at the one available Mass—scheduled
at bedtime. I had left All Saints Day Mass almost in tears
after an elderly parishioner—who, in fairness, had meant
well—had come all the way to the back to inform me
that everyone could hear the two-year-old up front, even

with the vestibule doors between us. I bit back the retort that I haven't been able to properly hear Mass in a half a decade. *What is the point?* I found myself bitterly asking God as we drove home, the kids nodding off to sleep in their car seats.

I know a lot of parents who have all but given up the idea of praying around children. As a first-time mom, I once reached out to an online Catholic mom's group for ideas on how to pray amid all the distractions, only to get cynicism. "Oh, you basically can't," one mom glibly informed me. Another just laughed at the thought. It turned out that many of the moms did not take their children to church, but traded Mass times with their husbands.

As a new mom, it was frightening to see how many women had effectively given up on the idea that a prayer life and motherhood were compatible. It was also depressing to hear—from well-intentioned women—ideas for how to simply *distract* children so that the adults could pray. It did not seem right—and it still does not—to distract children during prayer, and especially during the Church's corporate prayer of the Mass, rather than lead them—sometimes kicking and screaming—into a deeper appreciation of, and participation in, prayer.

Most of my mom friends are deeply committed to the heroic effort of praying with small children around. Even still, many are upset at the chaos of their spiritual life. "Mass this past Sunday was a disaster" is a common refrain. It is easy to sense that you lack a good daily prayer habit. It is easy to feel the loss of your former way of participating in Mass as a single person. But how to fix it?

There is often even a sense that your prayer life will show up eventually when you have time for it again—once the kids are grown and out of the house. As for the kids, well, let's hope they will grow into a prayer life when they are old enough. But sadly, only about 31% of Catholic parents of children younger than eighteen years old report having a daily prayer life.[86] I have the uncomfortable feeling that this is probably one of the major contributing factors to the rapid decline in religious practice in our society: many parents failed to cultivate an authentic prayer life because it is just so hard to feel like you are doing it right when children are involved. Not only are there so many distractions, but there is so little time in the day to set aside for meaningful prayer, either with our families or by ourselves.

By this, I am by no means implying that a fallen away Catholic is always the fault of parents who did not pray well when he or she was a child. There are many long-suffering Saint Monicas out there silently weeping for their errant children. But it is troubling just how many people I have met who, either actively or passively, fall into the assumption that a good prayer life is for people who do not have little children. And honestly, for every

---

[86]   Pew Research Center. "Frequency of Prayer among Catholics." 2014.

154 MOTHER TO MOTHER

one grump who looks askance at my children at church, there have been three elderly people who have thanked me for having my kids there . . . and they often sadly reflect that they wish that they had done the same back when their own children were small.

I think this stems from a mistaken understanding about prayer—we feel like we need to pray "correctly," the way that we did before we had kids, with opportunities for quiet focus and attention. If we spend the time designated for prayer, whether private prayer or the public prayer of the Mass, focused mostly upon our children and their distractions, it is easy to feel like we did not manage to pray at all. And with such discouragement, it is easy to fall into the trap of thinking bitterly, *what is the point?*

Fortunately, mothers are not the only ones who might have sighed out that worry when they were supposed to be praying. Saint Teresa of Ávila, Doctor of the Church and, as the Foundress of the Discalced Carmelite Reform, a professional prayer warrior, explains that what we might think of as perfect prayer is perhaps incorrect. In *The Interior Castle,* she explains,

> We err in thinking that we need only know that we must keep our thoughts fixed on Thee. . . . We pass through terrible trials, on account of not understanding our own nature and take what is not merely harmless, but good, for a grave fault. This causes the sufferings felt by many people,

particularly by the unlearned, who practice prayer. They complain of interior trials, become melancholy, lose their health, and even give up prayer altogether for want of recognizing that we have within ourselves as it were, an interior world. We cannot stop the revolution of the heavens as they rush with velocity upon their course, neither can we control our imagination. When this wanders we at once imagine that all the powers of the soul follow it; we think everything is lost, and that the time spent in God's presence is wasted. Meanwhile, the soul is perhaps entirely united to Him in the innermost mansions, while the imagination is in the precincts of the castle, struggling with a thousand wild and venomous creatures and gaining merit by its warfare. Therefore we need not let ourselves be disturbed, nor give up prayer, as the devil is striving to persuade us. As a rule, all our anxieties and troubles come from misunderstanding our own nature.[87]

What a beautiful image of prayer—and an important reminder that the attempt to pray can in fact be layered. Such that, perhaps unnoticed by ourselves, we are actually deeply united to God in the innermost chambers of ourselves while, on the ramparts, our imaginations can still do battle with those distractions outside, and the

---

[87]   Teresa of Avila, *The Interior Castle*. Robert Zimmerman, ed. (London: Thomas Baker, 1921), 41–42.

rest of our attention is focused on whatever it is our children need at the moment. Hopefully, in all this, we can become a model of prayer for those little eyes who are, in fact, watching us as we attempt to pray.

One of the most memorable moments of prayer I have ever had was when I was stuck in the back of church with a chattering toddler during a funeral service. This particular church was filled from floor to ceiling with icons. The toddler, long past the point of allowing me to focus on what was happening up front, was fascinated by the bright colors in the icons and wanted to touch all of the faces. We walked from face to face, pointing, whispering, naming the hosts of heaven and saying little prayers to them as they smiled back at us from the walls and peered down at us from the ceiling. Was this a distraction from what we were supposed to be doing in church? I think not. After all, two thousand years of Church Tradition has gloried in painting these images on every available space in the church building. Were they only meant to be examined in the few moments before or after the liturgy as we found our seats? We were praying in the only way that we, a mom and a toddler, could. But we were praying together, and we were there, engaged in our little way, in the corporate prayer of the Church, united with all of those saints all over the walls.

Question

One thing I and many fellow moms face is a sense of failure in prayer, because it is so easy to feel like we didn't do it "right." There are constant interruptions, mostly from young children who cannot or will not keep focused and make it hard for us to focus on prayer as well. I know that prayer does not have to be perfect to "count," but could you share some perspective on this?

Answer by Sister Anne Marie, Cistercians of the Valley of Our Lady

Try to not pass judgment on your prayer. What you see as your worst time of prayer—the most distracted and interruption-filled—may be the prayer that touches God most profoundly. We really cannot know. Those moments here and there where a "holy" gratitude for your husband and your children rushes into your heart are God's gift. These moments are prayer at its best, but it is God who gives it.

All we can do is thank Him when these moments come and long for them (desire them, and in desiring them, desire Him) when they are not present. There is also the prayer that comes erupting from us in moments when we realize our great need for God and His help. This prayer should be simple, direct, and humble: "Jesus, please help me!"

Question

One of the biggest myths that nuns tell me we laity hold is the idea that you spend all day in the chapel praying. You are busy about life in community as well! Obviously, moms cannot spend a lot of time praying in church throughout the week. I often spend Sunday Mass trying and failing to keep kids quiet and focused, and there are whole Masses where I feel like I've not managed to actively participate in a single prayer! But is there a way to pray while going about managing the tasks of life? What is your favorite way to pray "on the go"?

Answer by Sister Clare, Capuchin Sisters of Nazareth

Religious Life is conditioned to foster silent prayer throughout the day. Yet still, there are times when concentrating on the Mysteries of the Rosary or dialoguing familiarly with the Lord seem nearly impossible! This is when ejaculations come in handy! Short, sweet, and penetrating prayers from the heart serve to draw our minds and hearts upward, but don't distract us from our responsibilities in the moment. Prayer isn't about the words, but about the *love* in the prayer. Quite often, I find that different phrases move me personally in a deeper way at different times. For instance, sometimes it is, "Jesus, I trust in you!" Or when I sense I am anxious or worried, "I surrender all to you, Jesus." Other times it is, "My God, I love you," or "Jesus, Mary, I love you; save souls!" A powerful one, that can be difficult to pray when things aren't going as planned is, "Jesus, thank you for everything," or "Your will be done."

Once, I prayed the Name of Jesus over and over on a twenty minute drive to the eye-doctor. I met someone there who opened up and explained how he was a fallen away Catholic. I was then able to invite him back to the Lord. Leaving there, I knew that praying Jesus's Holy Name had straightened the way for this man and caused graces to flow during that encounter. I sensed that this conversation may not have taken place had I not prayed on the way there.

Ejaculations are powerful, especially in moments of temptation. They act as darts against the enemy and cause our will to refocus on the Lord as if we were telling him, "I don't want this sin, I want you, Lord."

Since the sky is the limit when it comes to these little prayers, I very often will ask the Lord in the morning for a phrase that He wants me to repeat to Him that day. Perhaps it comes to me in the Scriptures or Mass, or a meditation I read, or even in the lyrics of a song I can't seem to get out of my head! Everything can become a prayer! Even when words fail us, it can be our very actions, our intentions, *our love* that makes our prayers. Let each day's duties (every meal you cook, every child's embrace) *be* your prayer, because Jesus Himself told us, "As you did it to one of the least of these my brethren, you did it to me" (Mt. 25:40).

God does not want our words as much as He wants our very hearts! When we do everything for love of Him, there is no greater gift He can ask of us. Let us unite ourselves to Him with love in every action, and thus our prayer will be unceasing!

Answer by Mother Abbess
Cecilia, Benedictines

Mother Mary Francis told a funny story of a Poor Clare being asked by her mother, "Darling, what do you do all day?" When the nun proceeded to outline the daily schedule, the mother replied, "But darling, how do you do it all in a day?" It is true, there is a great deal that has to be done in order to keep a monastery going. We do have set hours of prayer, and these powers of prayer are meant to flow into the work.

Saint Benedict was very wise to have us chant the Divine Office for so many hours of the day. He acknowledged the power of music and the very human tendency to get songs stuck in your head. So it is that we chant the office, in the hopes that the music and its inspired texts will accompany us in work throughout the day.

We cannot remain in prayer for the whole of the day to the same degree. Father Hardon compares prayer to motherhood. Mental prayer is a bit like when the mother has some one-on-one time with the baby, where all her attention is focused on the baby and his beauty and God's gift to her. During work hours, prayer is more like a mother having to prepare a meal while listening for the baby in the next room. This is the extent of recollection that God expects from us. There is work to do. "You can't eat an alleluia," a Benedictine monk once said. It is true. Bread must be provided.

People do not often have the luxury of spending many hours at prayer, and the times allotted can be distracted. However, we must remember that the whole point of prayer is to be conformed to God's will. This is what union with God essentially means, being united with His will. Saint Benedict says that the guest is to be welcomed as Christ. Most of us thought this had to do with how well the guests should be treated. In reality, it means that Christ is to be sought in the guest, that God's will is to be sought in the welcoming of a guest, even if it is during a time of prayer.

The same can be said of a mother trying to hear Mass while her children are misbehaving. God's will is in embracing the opportunity for patience, rather than our preference of peaceful, uninterrupted prayer. God's will is most important. We pray so as to have our will be one with God. If His world calls us away from prayer, then so be it. It is God's will that will make us saints.

Saint John of the Cross's Prayer of Peace

O Blessed Jesus, grant me stillness of soul in Thee. Let Thy mighty calmness reign in me. Rule me, O thou King of gentleness, King of peace. Give me control, control over my words, thoughts and actions. From all irritability, want of meekness, want of gentleness, O dear Lord, deliver me. By thine own deep patience give me patience, stillness of soul in Thee. Make me in this, and in all, more and more like Thee. Amen.

CHAPTER 13

Fostering Love

"Love is patient and kind; love is not jealous or
boastful; it is not arrogant or rude. Love does not
insist on its own way; it is not irritable or resentful;
it does not rejoice at wrong, but rejoices in the right.
Love bears all things, believes all things, hopes all
things, endures all things . . . Love never ends."

—1 Cor 13:4–8

There is a poem that has stuck with me for over a decade, since I first stumbled upon it late one evening while flipping through an anthology of American poetry. It is by a poet named Robert Hayden, who wrote a poem about his father called "Those Winter Sundays." Even if you are not a poetry person, you should read it:

Sundays too my father got up early
and put his clothes on in the blueblack cold,
then with cracked hands that ached
from labor in the weekday weather made
banked fires blaze. No one ever thanked him.

I'd wake and hear the cold splintering, breaking.

When the rooms were warm, he'd call,

and slowly I would rise and dress,

fearing the chronic angers of that house,

Speaking indifferently to him,

who had driven out the cold

and polished my good shoes as well.

What did I know, what did I know

of love's austere and lonely offices?[88]

The poem is about love, but it is not a feel-good sort of love. It is about a love that works alone, behind the scenes, unacknowledged and unthanked. Only years later does the son recognize his father's self-sacrifice and quiet love for what it is. I especially love how the poem focuses on Sunday: a day when the father could have slept in and taken his rest, but instead finds him polishing his son's good shoes for church.

Fostering love within the community of the home is at the core of our task as parents, and especially as mothers, sometimes by doing our own "austere and lonely offices," unseen and unthanked. There are some things that my own mother did for us as children that I never noticed until I became a mother myself. Interesting how, years

88   Robert Hayden, "Those Winter Sundays," *The Norton Anthology of American Literature,* Eighth Edition, Volume E. Nina Baym, and Robert S. Levine, eds. (New York: W.W. Norton and Co., 2012), 172.

after the fact, you can suddenly catch sight of the quiet sacrifices of others. It makes me wish I could go back in time and adjust some childish responses to what was clearly an office of love: things that were "just" chores, or worse, annoyances of home life that were, unknown to my child eyes, the very cords of love that underpinned the home itself . . . What did I know, indeed! What did I know?

Fostering love within our little communities is of course not simply a quiet and lonely affair. After all, the heart of a mother is the heart of the home. Psalm 128, which describes the blessings that shall visit a faithful man, proclaims that, "Your wife will be like a fruitful vine within your house; your children will be like olive shoots around your table."[89] A fruitful vine in the center of the home, its branches and tendrils shooting out to cover the walls and roofs, weaving everything together in lush beauty. Is there anything more inviting or more delicious than such an image?

But lest we mothers get too comfortable with such a glorious image of our role, the reverse is true. Is there anything more damaging to a family than a mother who does not attempt to foster love, who neglects those austere offices? I have a vivid memory of a conversation with a colleague from graduate school. The two of us were attempting to pass the time on a dull stretch in the college writing center one afternoon, talking about

---

[89]   Ps 128:3.

our childhoods. In the middle of the usual sort of back-and-forth story swapping, my acquaintance paused. She was trying to sort something out in her head, wanting to make sure that it came out right before she said it.

"My mom gave me a good example . . . of what a successful woman looks like," she finally said. It turned out that her mother was not in any of her good memories of childhood. Her mother had been too busy with her career, her interests, her goals. The good example that the girl was referring to was how her mother had honed her focus and refused to allow distractions—including her children—to get in the way of her personal goals. My companion never said it, but her face communicated much more than the carefully chosen words: her mother had not cultivated love in the family home. The end product was a young woman who had buried the hurt, the loneliness, and the lost love so deeply that she was attempting to depict, in a positive light, her mother's failure to tend to love's offices.

Many people have mothers who fled from the task of fostering love in their families and communities. It is, sadly, a product of this fallen world. And it can happen to any sort of mother, even those of us who have chosen to stay home for the express purpose of tending the fires of domestic love. All-too-often, we can let the chore list hold pride of place, forgetting in the rush to get it all done to do it all with love, in love, and for love.

Love itself can be difficult, for it takes so much time, practice, and attention. With all of my best intentions for a joyful, love-filled day with my children, I find myself snapping at one or another of them or glancing down at something interesting on my phone only to look back up and discover that I have missed an opportunity to engage and cultivate love. But is any of it worth doing, if not for love?

Saint Mother Teresa of Calcutta, addressing the World Conference on Women in Beijing, 1994, expressed this most powerfully:

> God has created each one of us, every human being, for greater things - to love and to be loved. But why did God make some of us men and others women? Because a woman's love is one image of the love of God, and a man's love is another image of God's love. Both are created to love, but each in a different way. Woman and man complete each other, and together show forth God's love more fully than either can do alone.
>
> That special power of loving that belongs to a woman is seen most clearly when she becomes a mother. Motherhood is the gift of God to women. How grateful we must be to God for this wonderful gift that brings such joy to the whole world, women and men alike! Yet we can destroy this gift of motherhood, especially by the evil of abortion, but also by thinking that other things like jobs or positions

are more important than loving, than giving one-self to others. No job, no plans, no possessions, no idea of "freedom" can take the place of love. So anything that destroys God's gift of motherhood destroys His most precious gift to women—the ability to love as a woman.[90]

Question

A problem I have noticed among moms is that our husbands often end up getting the short end of the stick when it comes to our attention. Our babies need us, our grade-schoolers have homework that won't figure itself out, and those dishes in the sink needed doing days ago. There's a rather bitter joke I've heard more than once— that we'll spend time with our husbands once the kids move out. Now, another joke I've heard is that nuns have the best of all possible worlds: with Christ as your bridegroom, you don't have all the issues we lay wives have with ours! But you spend so much time with your bridegroom. I have a feeling that you do that not just because He is your God but because He is your spouse, and spouses need more than the short end of the stick, even the Divine spouse! Can you share your thoughts on this?

---

[90]   Mother Teresa of Calcuta, "Message to Fourth World Con-ference on Women." September 5, 1994. https://www.crossroads initiative.com/media/articles/mother-teresas-message-to-4th -womens-conference/ October 14, 2020.

Answer by Mother Marija, Byzantine Carmelites

Well, she didn't produce the kids by herself! And it is an ongoing process to have children together! But a woman's power is very great. It is how she uses it that matters. I believe that the greatest enabler of love is respect. You know that if someone respects you, they can move on to love you. And so, love is fragile because respect is its foundational stone. Also, children must see their parents' respect for each other.

A mother can do a great deal if she does this. I think the important thing for anyone is to be conscious of what God has given them to do. And then do the job they are given. I am the master of long stories . . . Years ago, we had a young mother nearby who had just had twins, and she had three other children. Then her husband got very sick, and they were having financial difficulties from this. She happened to be a third order Carmelite, and so she asked for time off from the meetings, which she could not manage in addition to her familial duties. Unfortunately, she was required to opt out instead—a decision that the leaders later realized was wrong. However! Perhaps it was the decision that God wanted. I can see how little explosions in our lives lead to other things. We see explosions and burnt fingers, but God may see a great future. Now, she leads a Myrrh Bearing Group (an Eastern lay women's apostolate) that is spread across the whole country. I am amazed.

What I am saying is this: your primary vocation is the first and most important thing. When this woman's husband got sick, she gathered the kids around her and they committed, as a family, to join him in his medically required diet. She did the full fasting with him, and the children, as much as they were able. It fostered such a solidarity in their family. Her husband adores her; she could do anything now, and he would support it!

In the vocation of marriage, you marry each other. The priest doesn't marry you: you do. And that's what it is all about. Look at the Little Flower's family, at her mother and her father. Two canonized saints! I was at their canonization, and they were canonized as a couple. That's the big thing: *together.*

Answer by Sister Clare, Capuchin Sisters of Nazareth

Religious *are* spouses of Jesus Christ. And so, everything that we do is for love of Him. He knows this, even if we don't tell Him so, but He loves to hear it all the same. Plus, it reminds *us* of our true motive for the smallest details of our life. Nevertheless, it would not be acceptable if we only *did things* for Him; He desires that we also *be* with Him. Religious have the advantage, so to speak, because we literally have our Husband with us 24/7—"I am with you always."[91] Yet, if we are always busy while with our Spouse, He will inevitably feel that these other things are more important

---

[91]   Mt 28:20.

than Him. God knows our hearts, but a human being cannot read them. I would imagine that, just as a religious *needs* the solitary times of intimate prayer, a heart-to-heart with her God, so too a wife must have time *alone* in intimacy with her husband. Perhaps, her being more conscious of *his* need for time with her would serve them both. A man's love is fixed on his wife while the wife's love is fixated on her children. Though she loves her husband, she is not as aware of his needs as she is for her children's, which are often more pressing, demanding, and obvious. A benign husband may not express his desire to be alone with his wife, but it is something God has placed within him in order to keep alive the spousal love. That is the bond of any marriage. Maybe the wife and mother's primary role is to *surrender more and more* to this loving pleading of her spouse. This is true of a spouse of Christ; it may also serve to strengthen the foundations of a family's love.

My own parents once told me that their love for each other (and joy in the other) grows every day! How does this happen? I know that it can only happen in religious life if I spend more quality time with my Spouse in deep prayer, if I make this the priority. My parents made the sixteenth of each month—their anniversary being on the sixteenth—their "date night," renewing their love and commitment to the other. They are extremely faithful to this, making sure they have that special time alone at a restaurant, on a walk, or at a movie. As a kid, I always looked forward to seeing how Dad's eyes would light up when Mom came out of the room all dressed up for the date. My parents would make holy hours together, periodically make a couple's retreat, and they always talked to each other at the dinner table each evening.

The parents' love for each other is essential, not only for themselves, but also for their children. It gives them a sense of security that nothing else can replace. They need to see this more than the laundry getting done or a fancy meal on the table. If the parents express joy in each other, the children will be happy. Of course, every vocation has its ups and downs, but the witness of forgiveness and reconciliation mutually given is the best example of Christian love for your children.

Lastly, "You will know them by their fruits."[92] If you and your husband strive to grow in holiness together (and individually), your children will absorb the graces to grow in holiness themselves. You cannot give what you do not have. If you want your children to be saints, first be saints yourselves. This is the goal of both marriage and of religious life: holiness.

Question

How do you create harmony and unity with radically different personalities? That is the beauty and the difficulty of family life—we don't get to pick the personalities that surround us in our home. There are often those two kids who just always rub each other the wrong way no matter

---

92   Mt 7:16.

what. A few of my mom friends have even confessed to me that they struggle to mesh well with the personality of one or more of their own children. I assume that this is true in the monastery as well. So how do you make it all work?

Answer by Sister Anne Marie, Cistercians of the Valley of Our Lady

Prayer is the most essential and the number one help for creating harmony and unity with radically different personalities. We acknowledge before God and to our own self that we are not the creator of harmony and unity. We are capable in our fallen human nature of creating disharmony and disunity, but harmony and unity come to us from God, and that is why prayer is the first and most essential tool we have at our disposal.

God asks us to love, and we know we can't, or at least, we know we are very poor at loving as He loves. Jesus instructs us to love those who hurt us.[93] A first step is to pray and do all we can with the Holy Spirit's help to not be the one doing the hurting. But we all know, sinners that we are, that we do sometimes fail, and our failures bring hurt to others. Most often, these failures on our part are not intended to hurt those around us, but that is usually the end result. In these situations, we pray and ask God to give the person we hurt the grace to forgive us, and in forgiving us, they are loving us. Loving those who hurt us can only be done with God's grace. We need

---

[93]   See Lk 6:27-28.

to pray and ask for that grace. Saint Augustine gives us this prayer: "Lord, give what you command, and command what you will."[94]

I have a dear friend in heaven, Blessed Maria Gabrielle. She lived about ninety years ago, so I did not know her. She is a Cistercian nun who offered her life to God for the unity of the Church. Soon after making this offer, she contracted tuberculosis. After a short time of great suffering, she died. She was in her twenties. I find when I turn to her for help in times of disunity, she responds with help from heaven.

Prayer to Saint Anthony of Padua, Protector of Lovers and Marriages

O Holy St. Anthony, gentlest of Saints, your love for God and charity for His creatures made you worthy, when on earth, to possess miraculous powers. Encouraged by this thought, I implore you to obtain for me (request).

O gentle and loving St. Anthony, whose heart was ever full of human sympathy, whisper my petition into the ears of the sweet Infant Jesus, who loved to be folded in your arms. The gratitude of my heart will ever be yours. Amen.

---

[94]   Augustine of Hippo, *Confessions.* Henry Chadwick, translator. (Oxford: Oxford University Press. 1998), 202.

CHAPTER 14

Temptations
and Failures

"A man would do nothing if he waited until he
could do it so well that no one could find fault."

—Saint John Henry Cardinal Newman

Two of Western Christendom's greatest saints are
Saint Augustine of Hippo and Saint Thomas Aquinas. Famously, Saint Augustine became a saint largely due
to the prayers and nagging of his mother, Saint Monica.
If not for Monica, Augustine would have ended up just
another victim of his own appetites instead of one of the
foremost theologians and saints of the Church. Father-
ing a child out of wedlock and abandoning his Christian
faith in pursuit of fame and pleasure, Augustine describes
his younger self in fairly bleak terms in his *Confessions*.
Famously, he records the flippant prayer of his youth:
"Give me chastity and continency, only not yet!"[95] But,
reflecting on God's presence in his life, even in his most

---

95   Augustine of Hippo, *Confessions*. Henry Chadwick, translator.
(Oxford: Oxford University Press. 1998), 145.

errant and sinful moments, Augustine would say, "whose words were they but yours which you were chanting in my ears through my mother, your faithful servant?"[96]

By contrast, Saint Thomas Aquinas, if he had listened to his mother, would have been anything but the Angelic Doctor. His parents, and especially his mother, Theodora, were horrified by the nineteen-year-old Thomas's embrace of the Dominican Order, and they had his brothers literally kidnap him on his way to the priory. His mother then imprisoned him in one of the family castles for over a year, nagging him to give up his vocation. She even hired a prostitute to tempt him—and Thomas famously responded by chasing the woman out of the room with a flaming log from the fire! In a holy rage, he then burned the image of a cross into the wall with that same log. Angels appeared to him, praising him for his commitment to chastity. Finally, to save face, his mother arranged for him to escape from a window late one night so that she would never have to admit defeat to Thomas, the Dominicans, and God.

Two of the greatest saints of the Church, and two very different mothers. For all of her faithfulness, Saint Monica was burdened with a son who caused her nothing but tears for decades before the miracle of his conversion. A holy bishop, seeing her weep for her wayward son, remarked, "It cannot be that the son of these tears

---

[96]   Augustine, *Confessions*, 27.

should perish."[97] By contrast, the young Thomas's faithful endurance and unassailable virtue was not taught by his failure of a mother. By rights, you would think that Saint Monica would produce Saint Thomas as her son, while having Theodora for a mother might explain a pre-conversion Augustine. But that is not always how it happens.

Obviously, mothers should strive to be more like Saint Monica and hope for sons who follow after Saint Thomas rather than take our chances with a young Augustine! But remembering Augustine and Thomas and their mothers together is important for those moments when we, our spouse, our children, or our family fail to live up to the ideal or cave to temptation. After all, Saint Thomas's halo is not shinier than Saint Augustine's from where they sit side by side in heaven.

Mothers can store up a lot of guilt about their failures—so much so that it has become a cliché. And it is obvious why: not only is our parenting supposed to craft emotionally and physically healthy adults, which is difficult enough, but, as Christians, we are also in charge of fostering their souls. While it is a glorious honor to be chosen as God's sub-creator, crafting His children for eternity, it is also terrifying; for we are very fallen craftswomen, and the weight of the potential consequences of our missteps is enough to keep anyone up at night.

---

[97]   Augustine, *Confessions*, 51.

In the spiritual letters of Abbot Chapman, OSB, the abbot remarks to a young layman:

> It is not necessary to "want God and want nothing else." You have only to "want to want God, and want to want nothing else." Few get beyond this really! But God is loving, and takes not only the will for the deed, but the will to will, or the wish to will. Consequently, I can't help advising you to pray. But when it goes badly, it goes well; for it becomes a continued humiliation: "Oh my God, you see I can't pray, I can't even desire, I can't keep my attention, etc." The great thing is union with God's Will; hence one can pass the time in accepting one's own baseness and incapacity. . . . It is one long act of love—not of my love to God, but of His to me. It is always going on—but in prayer you put yourself into it by an act of faith.
>
> The only thing that matters is *now*. I mean that we have to be exactly in God's Will—united actively and passively with what He has arranged for us to be and to do, so that at every moment we are quite simply in touch with God, because we are wishing to do what He wants of us, and to be as we find He wishes us to be. There is no other perfection than this. Tomorrow and yesterday are quite of secondary importance.[98]

---

[98]   Abbot John Chapman, *Spiritual Letters* (London: Burns & Oats, 2003), 46.

Question

If you are in a high-pressure moment during the day: you have dealt with lack of sleep, difficult people, and you just have a moment of extreme pressure and fatigue . . . how do you get through that pitfall where you are likely to fall into your bad habit (junk food or turning on the TV or just going to go hide in the bathroom)? This happens almost daily. I know it is partly the noonday devil, and it seems like it should be easy—just do not do that, go pray instead. But it is so hard sometimes. I need the right perspective on this.

Answer by Mother Marija, Byzantine Carmelites

Do not worry about just how exactly your family or life should look like. It will happen, but don't plan it. God is the master craftsman, and we are placed in His great mosaic. You should only plan a tiny little bit! He knows what He wants. Every day, something will happen that is His will. Sometimes, it is health-related! Or perhaps your husband loses his job today. We cannot make a plan for everything! But we can adjust ourselves to God's plan and count on His help. That, we can do, and it's really the strength we need. In our faith, there is a steadiness in our day and our life, and that is God.

So, we do not have to plan a great deal. We do have to be sure every day that we are reading the right recipe or are at the right gasoline tank! But count on Him. God will come because He wants us more than we want Him. And what He wants is our success—that we all get to heaven. I hope, that when I come before Him, I can say, "Lord, I'm something like what you wanted when you first started making me." That is really where our happiness lies.

You obviously have to do what is necessary to be done in a particular situation, but you do not have to get distraught about it. Well, at least, do not be distraught the next day! We sometimes have to be distraught in the moment—we do have to be human, right? We cannot deny ourselves our humanity. But we cannot arrogate to ourselves divinity. Do not try to plan His part.

When you trust God, then you put the worry and burden on Him. And if He doesn't want it, I don't want it, either. We do really have to say that, and we must mean it.

Question

Scrupulosity for a mother is a cliché—some of us are driven to distraction about tiny behaviors, habits, or failures that we have obsessively linked to our children's well-being, growth, and development. I can't tell you how many times I have panicked that I am ruining my children over something that my husband rightly reminds me is not a big deal in the grand scheme of things. While I am sure a nun's temptation to scrupulosity looks quite different than mine, I do want to know how you handle it. How can you tell if something is scrupulosity? How can we work on holding our scrupulosity in check?

Answer by Mother Abbess
Cecilia, Benedictines

Scrupulosity is extremely common among contemplatives, especially young ones. One of the most difficult facts with which to wrestle is that God has given us free will. Sometimes we wish we could be exempted from free will, that He would forestall all our bad actions, because, after all, the religious thinks, "I have given My life to Him. Therefore, even the tiniest things are huge in His eyes, especially as I live in such close quarters with Him, even under the same roof!"

This is overlooking the great truth that He is our Spouse. A perfect one, but our Spouse nonetheless, who seems to have an infinite capacity for mercy. I cannot tell you how many times a scrupulous sister comes to me with a scruple. So often, they are silenced by the question: "Do you really think He is going to condemn you to hell for this?"

It is too easy to be a control freak, even with God. This is the root of worrying. We are trying to avoid the suffering that God is allowing us to face in the fallen world, which He Himself has entered. He did not avoid but rather embraced suffering to show us how. Scrupulosity moves along the same vein as worry, except it makes us a control freak over God, trying to be the judge of our own souls. We forget that He said He is the life, and that He came that we might have life and have it more abundantly. Once the soul is grounded in humility, it can receive the love of God personally. It can step back and let God be

God over circumstances that cause us pain and even over our own souls, and let itself be loved instead, as St. Elizabeth of the Trinity says.

Question

How do you know if you are encountering a spiritual attack when you are depressed or stressed or things are just getting to you, and when it is just you letting the pressures of everyday life get to you? Or is there a difference?

Answer by Sister Anne Marie, Cistercians of the Valley of Our Lady

Ultimately, it may not matter a whole lot whether it is a spiritual attack or just letting the stress and pressures of everyday life get to you. What we do know is that the devil is like a prowling lion looking for someone to devour. The devil, seeing on our countenance the look of one who is feeling down, knows that is the best point of entrance and will take advantage of it. So, how does one avoid feeling depressed or stressed? I might offer a few possible helps:

a) Step back and quietly say, "this too will pass."
b) Step back and think of and annunciate to yourself ten blessings in your life, and maybe start with your Catholic faith.
c) Aspirations (short prayers) to the rescue!
d) Try to take a more deliberate notice of the beauty of a child's (your child's) eyes and face.

Prayer of Saint Germanus, as recorded by Saint Alphonsus Liguori in *The Glories of Mary*[99]

Oh my only Lady, who art the sole consolation which I receive from God; thou who art the only celestial dew that doth soothe my pains; thou who art the light of my soul when it is surrounded with darkness; thou who art my guide in my journeyings, my strength in my weakness, my treasure in my poverty; balm for my wounds, my consolation in sorrow; thou who art my refuge in misery, the hope of my salvation, graciously hear my prayer, have pity on me, as is befitting the mother of a God who hath so much love for men. Thou who art our defense and joy, grant me what I ask; make me worthy of enjoying with thee that great happiness which thou dost enjoy in heaven. Yes, my lady, my refuge, my life, my help, my defense, my strength, my joy, my hope, make me to come with thee to paradise. I know that, being the mother of God, thou canst obtain this for me if thou wilt. Oh Mary, thou art omnipotent to save sinners, thou needest nothing else to recommend us to thee, for thou art the mother of true life.

---

[99] Saint Alphonsus Liguori, "Some Devout Prayers of Various Saints to the Holy Mother." In *The Glories of Mary*. New Revised Edition. P.J. Kenedy & Sons, New York. 1888. https://www.ecatholic 2000.com/liguori/glories.shtml.

CHAPTER 15

Attending to Our Own Needs

"Take care of your health, that it may serve you to serve God."

—Saint Francis de Sales

When my oldest was a toddler, she took a two-hour nap in the middle of every afternoon. Those two hours were, in my mind, absolutely sacrosanct. They were a time where I could finally focus on whatever it was that I needed that day. I loved spending time with my daughter, but those two hours were always a relief. Those were my two hours.

Then a few more kids joined that afternoon nap. I worked overtime to make sure that the naps all started— and hopefully stopped—at basically the same time. I needed those two hours. But then my oldest did not need a nap anymore, and in fact, as we started home-schooling, I realized that those two hours were prime candidates for quality time with the ABCs and math. But I did not want to give them up. I thought that I could not give them up. When would I tend to my own needs? I needed that time. . . .

Once, I was reading a spiritual fantasy novel by George MacDonald called *Lilith*. There is one scene where Lilith, an evil witch queen, has been brought to the brink of repentance by a long-repentant Adam and Eve. She wants to sleep the sleep of peace, but she cannot, for she is clutching something in her hand that she must give up first. She cannot bring herself to loosen her grip on that thing.

That image plagued me. I felt that I was holding those two hours of "me time" tightly in my own hand, disrupting the peace of my household. But I was afraid to let go and let that time slip from my fingers. How would I attend to my own needs? I gave my family every other hour of the day. . . .

Then one day, I felt my grip loosening. My daughter was really excited about her newfound reading skills and wanted quiet time when her siblings were asleep to share them with me. I let go of those two hours. I felt them slip out of my grasp and, to my surprise, I discovered that I did not actually need them. Maybe I had needed them as a brand-new wife and mother, but now, several years deeper into my vocation, I realized that I no longer did. I had grown out of those needs, and only discovered it once I was asked to let them go.

I think there is still quite a lot tightly gripped in my hand. Perhaps it is not yet time to give them up, but I am coming to the belief that part of the journey of Christian vocation is a gradual letting go of those personal things that we are holding on to. There are needs—truly valid needs—that I have now that one day, I will be asked to let go of and recognize that they are needs no longer. Hopefully, I will have the faith and humility to let them slip from my grasp as well. After all, Christ was clear about the requirements for His followers: "If any man would come after me, let him deny himself and take up his cross and follow me. For whoever would save his life will lose it, and whoever loses his life for my sake will find it."[100]

Fortunately, Christ knows us well enough to know that most of us need to answer that call gradually. Saint Paul promises us that God will never allow us to be tested more than we can handle.[101] Sometimes, I must admit that God has a much higher opinion of my abilities than I do! But just like a marble statue, I am being chipped away bit by bit, until the perfect saint He has envisioned is complete—that is, if I allow the unnecessary bits of me to be carved away; if I am able to let go when the time comes to surrender something I had thought was essential.

It is difficult to determine what are valid needs and what are things that we have grown out of and need to let go. I think mothers especially struggle with this, since we spend so much time answering to the needs of others.

---

[100]   Mt 16:24-5.
[101]   See 1 Cor 10:13.

Anne Morrow Lindburgh, wife of the famous aviator
Charles Lindburgh, frames the struggle to attend to our
needs in this way, "how to remain whole in the midst of
the distractions of life; how to remain balanced, no matter what centrifugal forces tend to pull one off center;
how to remain strong, no matter what shocks come in at
the periphery and tend to crack the hub of the wheel."[102]
She does not offer any easy answer to this question of
how to remain balanced, so that we can achieve inner
peace no matter what is going on outside. But she suggests a way that, when you think about it, is very much in
line with the contemplative vocation:

> To ask how little, not how much, can I get along
> with. To say—is it necessary?—when I am tempted
> to add one more accumulation to my life, when I
> am pulled toward one more centrifugal activity.
> Simplification of outward life is not enough. It is
> merely the outside. But I am starting with the out-
> side. I am looking at the outside of a shell, the out-
> side of my life—the shell. The complete answer is
> not to be found on the outside, in an outward mode
> of living. This is only a technique, a road to grace.
> The final answer, I know, is always inside.[103]

---

[102]   Anne Morrow Lindburgh, *Gift from the Sea* (New York: Pan-
theon Books, 1955, 2003), 18.
[103]   Anne Morrow Lindburgh, *Gift from the Sea*, 20-1.

Question

How and when should you ask for help? It is hard to know when I just need to offer it up and keep my mouth closed and my fingers busy at the task at hand, and when I genuinely need to seek the aid of others. I think this is a fear a lot of moms have—we don't want to be a burden to others and don't want to admit defeat, and so we suffer in silence when we should reach out for help.

Answer by Sister Anne Marie, Cistercians of the Valley of Our Lady

Maybe start with a simple practice for gaining a ten minute "retreat" here and there, especially when most needed: a) pause, b) step back, c) offer thanks, d) enjoy a cup of coffee or tea, e) call to mind your favorite Scripture verse or verses and sit with that as you slowly sip your coffee.

Now about a "need" to ask for help and the concern to not be a burden to others . . . If reaching out starts to become more and more frequent on your part, it may be perceived by those giving you help as a burden. One must look into her own heart to discern if this reaching out for help is becoming a kind of escape. On the other hand, if you know yourself to be one who rarely ever asks for help (for a break), and you come to a point where you are wondering whether or not you should ask for help, YES, ask for help. We need to avoid extremes. Saint Thomas instructs us that in the middle is virtue.

Try to know yourself and your tendencies. Are you more likely to slip into wanting to escape the demands of love placed on you day in and day out? If so, be on your guard and when in doubt, don't ask for help. If you are more likely to ignore your real need and be overly concerned about placing a burden on someone, you will want to be on your guard against ignoring what is in fact a real need. Sometimes, we hold back from asking for help because we fear getting the response, "I'm sorry, I can't help". Most often, you will know someone who would be only too happy to respond to your request for help if you were to simply ask.

Question

My mom spent a year in a convent before discerning out, and she said that while she was there, she was surprised at just how much cleaning nuns did around the place. As a mom and homemaker, I often feel like all I do is clean things. I know that is a huge struggle for a lot of moms . . . keeping things clean and the depressing feeling like we are just "the maid" of the household can really be a struggle. As cloistered nuns, you are sort of like God's homemakers, doing most of your work in and around the home of your monastery. Do you have any words of wisdom about how to reframe housework so that it feels like less of a chore and more part of our vocation?

Answer by Mother Mary Angela
and the Roswell Poor Clares

It is very helpful to reflect on Mary and her life at Nazareth. She was the "handmaid of the Lord" in every way, and she truly saw herself as servant and handmaid, without any loss of her dignity. She must have done a great deal of housework, and we can be absolutely certain that she did it with love, peace, and joy—no matter how tedious the actual work might have been. Housework is a very feminine thing—bringing order and beauty through the humble tasks of cleaning, sweeping, tidying, folding clothes, etc. We can bring Our Lady into the work through our prayer. We also think of dear St. Joseph, who was surely diligent and patient in fatigue.

The media has trivialized this kind of work—as if having a career is so much more important than caring for a home. The most important thing to do is the will of God, and if cleaning the home is His will, there's nothing better we can be doing!

Taking care of the house is a way of taking care of the family. But it's important that it does not become the top priority. We must be realistic—not everything is possible, and a *Better Homes and Gardens* type house probably won't happen anytime soon with small children. A priest once advised a housewife: get up in the morning and say, "I want to make this home a happy place to live!"

The Franciscan attitude towards work is a beautiful one. We see work as a *grace* and as contributing to our life of prayer. It is part of our Franciscan vocation to work hard.

One sister shared that Saturday morning was cleaning day for the whole family because this was the only time they were all together. She loved it because everything was clean and orderly at the end! This also helps the children learn sacrifice, even at a very young age, and to value cleanliness and order.

Bringing the children into the housework, teaching them how to clean, is also helpful on the practical level— they eventually become able to make a contribution. Turning cleaning into a kind of game, (cleaning a room together, each with an assignment). As soon as they are old enough, the children should have assigned chores. In the monastery, we have community workdays when we all work on some project together, cleaning or gardening, etc.—we look forward to these days when we are all working together!

It is the love behind it that matters. All the acts of sacrifice "go out" to help others, to build peace. Raising a family is sacrificial: God knew what He was doing when He started the family. It is all part of the offering; it is all part of making the gift of self as wife and mother more complete. This is a true vocation, a calling, and the grace is there to fulfill it *gracefully*.

Saint Junípero Serra: "To the willing heart, all things are sweet."

Saint John of the Cross: "Put love where love is lacking."
For us, the monastery is God's house, so we want it to
shine!

Question

*How do you find balance between answering the needs of
others, especially those in your community, and your own
needs? I often feel guilty when I stop to take care of myself,
because there are so many things and people who need me
as a mother. But then I end up feeling resentful of the very
people I am called to love the most, not because they have
done anything, but because I am failing at finding a good
balance. I don't want to feel guilty when I take a break, but
I am often unsure of what is a genuine need and what is a
selfish desire for more "me time."*

Answer by Mother Abbess
Cecilia, Benedictines

It is hard to find the balance of when to relax, but the
judge of this is charity. If you find yourself impatient and
unable to show the charity that God wants of you for
your family, this is the sign to do something. Charity is
the queen of virtues. When it is threatened, this is a sure
sign to take a break. If God requires something else of
you, He will make that known.

The important part is to let God take the driver's seat.
He does not like planners; He prefers when we are abandoned to His will. When duties become too much and

infringe on our ability to be patient and charitable, that is the time to reassess—weeding out selfish motives and reading the signs of one's own weakness.

The Litany of Humility

O Jesus! Meek and Humble of Heart, **Hear me.**

From the desire of being esteemed,
   Deliver me, Jesus.

From the desire of being loved, **Deliver me, Jesus.**

From the desire of being extolled, **Deliver me, Jesus.**

From the desire of being honored,
   Deliver me, Jesus.

From the desire of being praised, **Deliver me, Jesus.**

From the desire of being preferred to
   others, **Deliver me, Jesus.**

From the desire of being consulted,
   Deliver me, Jesus.

From the desire of being approved,
   Deliver me, Jesus.

From the fear of being humiliated,
   Deliver me, Jesus.

From the fear of being despised, **Deliver me, Jesus.**

From the fear of suffering rebukes,
   Deliver me, Jesus.

From the fear of being calumniated,
   Deliver me, Jesus.

From the fear of being forgotten, **Deliver me, Jesus.**

From the fear of being ridiculed, **Deliver me, Jesus.**

From the fear of being wronged, **Deliver me, Jesus.**

From the fear of being suspected, **Deliver me, Jesus.**

That others may be loved more than I, **Jesus, grant me the grace to desire it.**

That others may be esteemed more than I, **Jesus, grant me the grace to desire it.**

That, in the opinion of the world, others may increase and I may decrease, **Jesus, grant me the grace to desire it.**

That others may be chosen and I set aside, **Jesus, grant me the grace to desire it.**

That others may be praised and I unnoticed, **Jesus, grant me the grace to desire it.**

That others may be preferred to me in everything, **Jesus, grant me the grace to desire it.**

That others may become holier than I, provided that I may become as holy as I should, **Jesus, grant me the grace to desire it.**

Amen.

CHAPTER 16

Supporting Children in Their Vocations

"'Mary, Mother of Vocations, pray for us,'
should be our daily invocation."

—Father John Harden

"**N**ot doing something for God, but being someone for God is the most powerful testimony one can give to the preeminence and supereminence of God. In a sense it is a greater testimony than physical martyrdom, since this kind of witness is a matter not of an act but of a state."[104]

Isn't that the most common question adults ask children? "And what do you want to be when you grow up?" Nobody asks, "Who do you want to be?" That sort of question would just be too bizarre. My two-year-old would probably announce proudly that he will be a dinosaur, but my seven-year-old would probably fall

---

[104]   Mother Mary Francis, P.C.C., *Strange Gods Before Me* (Poor Clares: 2020), 43.

awkwardly silent and sidle away from the situation. Yet, it seems as if that is really the goal of what we, as mothers, are called to direct our children towards. At the end of the day, who cares what they *do*. Who they will *be* is everything.

But how do you raise a child to be, especially in a world that is screaming at us to get them started on doing something as early as possible? More importantly, how do you get them to be someone for God?

As a teen, I was often taken to religious vocation fairs that were designed like job fairs. This is a good idea in that teens who might be interested in a religious vocation are exposed to the vast array of religious orders and can hopefully find one that really sparks their interest on a personal level. However, I never saw them in that way. They felt like job fairs, plain and simple. I think this was my fault, not the fault of the organizers. I was not thinking about who I wanted to be. That was an unexamined question I was not even asking myself. At that age, I was simply thinking about what I wanted to do. However, that is the wrong approach to any vocation, whether religious or married, because a vocation is about molding yourself into a certain type of person, rather than performing certain job functions at set times.

I do not need to rehash the crisis in which the world finds itself: fewer and fewer people are answering the vocational call to be religious monks or nuns, sisters or friars, priests or deacons. Also, alarmingly, fewer and fewer people are answering the call to be faithfully married with children. How do we instill an openness to the call of a vocation into our children, and how do we help them on the path to answering that call?

There is no perfect answer to these questions because every vocation is a unique and personal calling from God to an individual, and because everyone has free will. Remember Saint Thomas Aquinas and his horrible mother! But there must be ways to bolster our children towards the discovery and fulfillment of their own vocations. Here in this final section, we have several suggestions for ways in which we might do this.

Question

How would you help young children experience God's love? There's a worry I have that my children might resent religion at times because it often comes to them in the form of long liturgies in church, the constant hushing and shushing from their parents, and the requirement to be respectful and attentive to something that they struggle to follow and do not intellectually comprehend. Obviously, bringing our children to church is the only way to develop the habit and the desire for active participation in the public life of the church, but do you have any thoughts about how to make God's love more apparent to them?

Answer by Mother Marija,
Byzantine Carmelites

The relationship between spouses, and the attitude they have toward each other, will affect their children and their children's vocations so much. This matters a great deal, because it is the first school for a young person.

I have known a lot of women since I joined in 1946! So now, when a young lady comes to us to try her vocation, I can always tell, without fail, what I can expect as her superior based upon the relationship that she has had with her mother. Was it trusting? Loving? One of my sisters comes from Slovakia, where they lived under communism. Her mother is an absolute saint, and they are so close. It is that relationship with her mother that enables her to care for others in the community.

Also, especially for a girl, the relationship with her dad tells me a lot. Will she have a natural capacity for marriage? The love for a man? In the same way, will she have a good start to her relationship with Our Lord Jesus Christ? That is the same. Whatever it is within our hearts, it is the same. For a person who has had a bad relationship with her dad, the Our Father is a painful prayer—a very painful prayer.

Mothers can do a great deal for their children, and especially their daughters. They should strive not to foster competition, but good relationships between themselves and their children, and between themselves and their spouse.

And my job, when a young woman comes to us, is mostly to listen. Will I hear something? It is like looking in the sand for a ring: some words that will tell me this is a keyword for her, one that will tell me something about her spiritual interiority. The whole essential key from her home is that it has been a home of faith; especially a home where a role model for the Faith has been found.

Everyone, not just nuns, is called to activate inner Faith. What does that mean, really? What does it mean, to really believe in God? To show, not just by our lives, but by our thinking, attitudes, decisions, that we are ruled by Faith. The best thing a parent can do is show her children that she is ruled by Faith.

Answer by Sister Clare, Capuchin Sisters of Nazareth

Young children more easily believe what they are told (especially when it comes to "unseen things") than do most educated adults. Children are ripe to receive mystery. This is one of the reasons Christ called His disciples to become like little children: they have faith. Yet this faith is so quickly drowned out by what is seen in the world as they grow up. The key is not in trying to keep them from seeing everything—it is to teach them how to see things; to have the eyes of faith.

Children experience joys and sorrows just like everyone else. In fact, they are often more honest and raw with expressing these with someone they trust because they are not yet self-conscious. This means, for example, that they haven't learned that screaming doesn't help matters, but that it also makes things worse for them and everyone else. Nevertheless, the docility of this age is very precious, and they are more easily *taught*. Parents are, of course, the primary teachers of their children, *especially* when it comes to faith and morals. Parents should never accede this honor and privilege to anyone else, unless absolutely necessary! The younger this faith-training starts, the better. Like learning a language, if little children can learn to see everything as coming from a Father in heaven who loves them, then all of life will be seen through this lens as though it is second nature. It is never too soon to start pointing out signs of God to them.

As to applying this practically, only God can inspire you in the moment with each individual child, but a few suggestions may be a starting point:

1. Teach your children to talk to God about everything. Help them set up a little prayer corner in their room with a little altar and an image of Jesus, Mary, or their favorite saints. This will be where they can go when they are upset, grateful, or want to be alone with God. This is not time-out or a punishment, this is simply a place for them to seek God in all situations. You may even suggest a little prayer for them to pray while there.

   A humorous example of this was when my little brother, John, was upset at his older brothers for teasing him. He complained to Mom who suggested he go in the other room and tell God about it. She also suggested he pray Jesus's words from the cross, "Father, forgive them, for they know not what they do."

John took her advice and, if one was listening, you could hear a six-year-old pouring out his heart to Jesus. It wasn't long before John returned to Mom with a radiant smile and said, "I did it! I did what you told me, Mom! I said, 'Father, forgive me, 'cuz I don't know what I'm doing!'"

No matter what prayer he made, John was able to let go of his hurt and move on.

2. Take your kids to Mass. Sit up front and tell them with whispered awe what is happening. This may be a scary thought if you know one of your children is particularly rambunctious, but maybe it is because he or she cannot see the beautiful mystery of the liturgy that is taking place! When we sat up front at church, we watched the priest and not the other kids misbehaving around us. We were not perfect, but it helped cut down on distractions.

3. Fill their lives with the *holy*. Make the lives of the saints a daily and exciting encounter for your children. Talk to them about the saints, about their Mother Mary, and about Jesus's sacrifice for them. Celebrate their feast days (the saint whom they are named after), and/or the day of their baptism. Another idea is to give them holy cards or medals of saints as rewards for good behavior or helpfulness.

4. Most important of all, your children must see their parents pray! Both mom and dad must give this example. Seeing parents take time alone with God, reading scripture, praying the Rosary, going to adoration, giving up something for Lent, etc., all have a lasting impact on the child. The child will see it as a necessary thing, not only for kids but for the adults as well. Children will want to imitate mom and dad for the better, and they will forever have this image in their memory of their parents on their knees.

Pray with your children to teach them, but do not neglect giving that witness of personal prayer to God. If you and your spouse are holy, God will do the rest for your children.

Question

I would be remiss if I did not ask you how mothers can help support our children in their vocations. What are some specific things that we can do to help foster our children's discernment?

Answer by Sister Anne Marie,
Cistercians of the Valley of Our Lady

Children are easily inspired. Read to them about people who lived their lives for others. You yourself will be their daily example of this. Encourage in them a spirit of self-giving and generosity. When you see some instance of self-sacrifice, point out to them how pleasing that is to God and to those around them.

If possible, it is good for children to have some acquaintance with priests and religious sisters. Help them understand that any life worth living will be a life of love and that love means living not for oneself but for God and others. There will be pain and struggle in everyone's life. However, the pain and suffering that comes because we love, is a suffering that carries with it a deep joy from the Holy Spirit. To want a life of ease, one in which I give myself to no one, is to live with a cold emptiness that most often brings with it the deepest loneliness and despair.

God's call to follow Him in religious life is just that: a call, an invitation. The call is a grace and to respond to God with a yes is also a grace. This call may cause apprehension to rise up in one's heart, but that is completely normal. It is also true that the call brings a deep joy. For the most part, God does not give one hundred percent certainty about the call, because then one does not have to step out in faith. However, He does provide all the necessary graces, and to follow Him does not mean you are throwing your life away, nor does it mean you will live in sadness and misery. God does not call us to be miserable.

Pray for your children that they will come to know and follow the path in life God desires for them. This will be the path in which their lives will bless all those around them.

Question

Have you noticed any trends in the vocations that have come to your monastery in terms of family life? Is there something that we mothers can try to foster at home to help cultivate a religious vocation?

Answer by Mother Abbess
Cecilia, Benedictines

We are receiving a lot of vocations from families who homeschool. A homeschooled upbringing is a great help because one is in a family unit that closely resembles the monastery. There is more to do than just eat, sleep, and recreate together. One must learn together, too. The Armed Forces, as a workplace, shares this as well: there are going to be a variety of temperaments drawn together in a single mission, with little in common temperamentally or according to age. There are advantages to a classroom, but it is not natural to have so many people of the same age in the same place at the same time.

Now in a family, there is the advantage of being related, but there is also the danger of familiarity. It is true that familiarity breeds contempt. So too in the monastery, as religious life is called the life of the perfection of charity. That is a tall order, and we do not have the protection of all being related. We do have seven sets of sisters at the monastery, but these sisters must practice great detachment in favor of the whole.

Adaptability is the saving grace of every vocation. Eventually, the ideal is going to meet the real, and those from large, homeschool families already have a feel for that give and take of the family, similar to what we experience here at the monastery and the self-sacrifice required. There is nothing artificial about it. In general, the stronger the charity, the greater the discipline over one's own senses, and the greater the confidence one experiences from childhood, the surer the vocation will be. If one grows up knowing she is loved by her parents, she will assuredly believe in God's love for her.

Another major element that spells success in application is when one comes from a family where the father is thoroughly the head of the home. This makes a huge difference in the approach to obedience. If a child does not learn of the proper ordering of obedience from her parents, there will be a compromised sense of obedience in religious life. So, I encourage parents to be strong in their marital fidelity and submission to each other. Those who come from families that are well ordered in this way have a much easier time.

The *Angelus*

The Angel of the Lord declared to Mary:
And she conceived of the Holy Spirit.

Hail Mary, full of grace, the Lord is with thee; blessed art thou among women and blessed is the fruit of thy womb, Jesus. Holy Mary, Mother of God, pray for us sinners, now and at the hour of our death. Amen.

Behold the handmaid of the Lord:
Be it done unto me according to Thy word.

Hail Mary. . .

And the Word was made Flesh:
And dwelt among us.

Hail Mary. . .

Pray for us, O Holy Mother of God,
that we may be made worthy of
the promises of Christ.

Let us pray: Pour forth, we beseech Thee, O Lord, Thy grace into our hearts; that we, to whom the incarnation of Christ, Thy Son, was made known by the message of an angel, may by His Passion and Cross be brought to the glory of His Resurrection, through the same Christ Our Lord.

Amen.

CONCLUSION

Two Spiritual Mother Saints for Mothers

Not only can we lay mothers learn from the wit and wisdom of the spiritual mothers tucked away in the contemplative life all around us, but we can also look to the great spiritual mothers of the Church for guidance and prayers. Of course, due to a lot of factors, most of the canonized female saints in the past two thousand years and counting have been nuns. This is not because the Church does not recognize the saintliness of lay mothers, but because in order for a holy person's saintly recognition to gather steam, there has to be a dedicated group of people pushing for the would-be saint's canonization over the span of many years. No matter how amazing most mothers are, the very local, domestic focus of this vocation made it difficult over the centuries to gather and keep a crowd agitating the local bishop and then Rome for a declaration of sainthood. That is a great benefit of modern media: local cults of holy men and women can "go viral" in the Church in ways that were just not possible for all but the most famous saints of older times. It was, however, much easier for a monastery composed of a saintly nun's spiritual daughters and granddaughters to keep her cause going for as long as it took Rome to notice.

And while it is wonderful to have a growing number of lay women who are mothers and saints, it is also a great blessing to all Catholic mothers that we have centuries upon centuries of spiritual mothers whose wisdom and grace can still be deeply inspirational for us, although they led lives that, at least on the outside, were radically different than ours. In this final chapter, I would like to share with you two spiritual mothers of the Church—an ancient one and a modern one—who are relatively unknown to most Catholics. Their lives and their maternal care of souls might resonate with more modern mothers than one might think.

Saint Hilda, the Abbess of Whitby

The Venerable Bede, who wrote the first history of England long ago in the eighth century, tells us about Hilda, "All who knew her called her mother because of her outstanding devotion and grace." There is a lot about the details of Hilda's life that would be utterly alien to the experience of most women, much less modern mothers. However, a deeper look at her life shows us exactly what Bede meant when he wrote that beautiful line.

Born in England sometime in 614 AD, Hilda was the daughter of nobility, raised in the pagan household of her uncle, King Edwin. When Hilda was thirteen, Edwin's Christian wife, Æthelburh, finally convinced him and his entire court to be baptized in one huge ceremony on an Easter morning in a little wooden church that was built for the occasion. The only other fact we know about Hilda's early life is that she was close to Queen Æthelburh and was probably one of her ladies-in-waiting, helping the queen run the domestic side of King Edwin's courtly household.

Hilda's story picks up at age thirty-three, when she answered the call to become a nun. Quickly, Hilda became the abbess of the most important abbey in all of England: Whitby. Unlike most monasteries even in the Middle Ages, Whitby was really two monasteries in one; a male monastery stood nearby the female one, and the monks and nuns would meet daily for communal prayers and Mass. Hilda was elected the superior over both monasteries. Her organizational skills must have been extraordinary. Hilda received letters and even visits from kings and bishops who sought her advice on administrative and spiritual matters. Her abbey was even chosen as the spot where an important synod met to settle the contentious debate as to when Easter should be celebrated in England.

But she did not run her monasteries like tight, well-oiled machines. She ran them like spiritual households, taking personal interest in even the most humble of her spiritual children. She was devoted to the spiritual and personal well-being of all who came under her maternal authority. Most famously, there is the story of her spiritual son, Caedmon.

Caedmon was an illiterate peasant who joined the abbey of Whitby as a lowly lay brother and was assigned to take care of the sheep and cows. Whitby was famous for its sheep, which not only provided wool and meat, but also skins for vellum paper. This paper became the pages of magnificent, illuminated manuscripts made by the most skilled and learned monks. But Caedmon was only a humble shepherd.

One evening, on a feast day, the monks were celebrating by taking turns singing hymns and poetry that they had composed. Caedmon, who was untalented even at making music, was sad that he lacked the talent to compose beautiful sacred music like the monks. He was too painfully shy and uneducated. So, he snuck out early to hide away glumly in the cowshed with the livestock. In the middle of the night, he received a vision where a stranger stood before him and commanded him to sing about the beginning of all creation. Caedmon mumbled out that he did not know how and was no good at trying, but the stranger insisted. Finally, Caedmon tried, and the result, according to Venerable Bede, is the first English poem, a hymn praising the Creator of Creation.

When Hilda found out about the vision and Caedmon's hymn, she summoned him, and she listened to his story and his sudden magnificent talent for hymn-making. Sure, he was only the shepherd, and there were kings and bishops awaiting her wisdom, but Hilda took time for her spiritual son. She recognized both his beautiful gift and his deep-seated need: he needed to be taught more rigorously about theology so that his poetry could become even more inspirational for those who heard it. So, she made sure that her learned monks took time out of their busy days for the important task of educating and aiding their fellow brother. Caedmon then turned all that he learned into magnificent songs that sounded out all around the countryside.

Hilda is a perfect model for the busy mother who has been called to wear many hats. Each honor, each important responsibility, each new task to oversee never distracted Hilda from her primary role as a mother to her many spiritual children. She was a woman of grace and devotion, and all who knew her called her "mother."

Saint Hilda's feast day is November 17th. She is the patroness of learning and culture, but I think she would be a good patroness for mothers of gifted children, special education children, homeschool mothers, working mothers, and mothers who struggle to stay organized!

Caedmon's Hymn[105]

Now let us praise Heaven-Kingdom's guardian,

the Maker's might and His mind's thoughts,

the work of the glory-father—of every wonder,

eternal Lord. He established a beginning.

---

[105] Caedmon, "Caedmon's Hymn." Roy M. Liuzza, translator. https://www.poetryfoundation.org/poems/159193/caedmon39s-hymn.

He first shaped for men's sons
Heaven as a roof, the holy Creator;
then middle-earth mankind's guardian,
eternal Lord, afterwards prepared
the earth for men, the Lord almighty.

Saint Maravillas de Jesus

Saint Maravillas de Jesus was a wonderful woman—and
her name itself means "Wonders." Born on November 4,
1891, and entering eternal life on December 11, 1974, Maravillas is a spiritual mother of modern times whose story
reads as impressively as a wonder-working ancient saint.

Born into a very pious family in Madrid, Maria de las
Maravillas was named after Our Lady of Wonders. Her
father was a politician and served for a time as the Spanish ambassador to the Holy See. Maravillas's vocation
was fostered from an extremely early age by her widowed
grandmother, who had taken a vow of poverty and lived
as a sort of contemplative almsgiver. Her grandmother
would take her to visit different religious orders, and the
two would visit the poor of Madrid together.

Maravillas longed to become a Carmelite and begged
her parents to let her join a monastery, but despite
their deeply held faith, her parents could not bear the
thought of their daughter leaving them for a cloister and
refused to let her go. However, after her father's death
when she was nineteen, her mother finally relented,

and Maravillas entered the El Escorial Discalced Carmel, taking the religious name Maravillas de Jesus (The Wonders of Jesus).

When a woman enters a Carmelite monastery, she assumes that she will live and die within those four walls, since Carmelites follow the strictest form of cloistered life. However, God had other plans for Maravillas. When she was still a novice, she felt a burning calling to found a new Carmel in the geographical heart of Spain, the Cerro de los Angeles. The Cerro was a mountain with a crumbling shrine to the Sacred Heart. Normally, a novice asking to become a foundress would not be taken seriously, but Maravillas's discerning superiors realized that this was a call from God and let her go, taking a couple of sisters with her. Maravillas began answering a radical call to motherhood that would result in the founding of over twenty Carmels in Spain, and even sending a few of her spiritual daughters to found Carmels in India.

When they arrived at the Cerro, there was no place to live. Two years later, when the new Carmel was dedicated by the bishop, Maravillas made her final profession and was appointed prioress. In her diary, she wrote the words of Christ to her about the Cerro Carmel: "Here I want you and those other souls chosen by my Heart to make me a house where I have my delight. My Heart needs to be consoled and let this Carmel which I want be a balm that heals the wounds that sin makes in me. Spain will be saved by prayer."

Women flocked to the Cerro and to Mother Maravillas. However, the Spanish Civil War broke out on their very doorstep, and Maravillas and her spiritual daughters were forced away from their home by communists. They were loaded onto a bus to be taken away and shot, but God changed the heart of the bus driver, who instead dropped them at a ramshackle apartment in the city. Maravillas and her sisters fled to the Salamanca desert and reached the ruins of a medieval monastery, where Saint John of the Cross had once lived. They spent the next few years rebuilding the ruins into a functioning Carmel.

Even in such difficult surroundings, Maravillas's reputation as a spiritual mother was renowned. So much so that she received a great flood of vocations and had to keep building new Carmels to fit all the religious. Maravillas was a faithful daughter of Saint Teresa of Ávila and made sure that each Carmel she built remained "family sized" as the great Carmelite reformer had wanted. This meant that sometimes, just as soon as a monastery was dedicated, Maravillas and two other sisters would depart for another grassy field to start building another Carmel.

Maravillas wanted nothing more than to be a simple nun, staying forever in one Carmel, but she never said no to the plans of God—and God wanted her to build Him so many homes! She even managed to return to her original Cerro monastery, which had been razed to the ground by the communists. There were no workmen to assist the rebuilding, so Maravillas and her nuns did the work themselves.

In the 1960s, liberalism, masquerading as reform, saw thousands of nuns abandon their traditions, charisms, and even vocations. But not Maravillas. She had suffered too much for her beloved vocation and had guided too many young women to their own vocations to be fooled by all the chatter. Her deeply maternal wisdom guided her and her spiritual daughters through the attempts to liberalize the Discalced Carmelite order. She founded an association of Carmels committed to the traditions handed down from Saint Teresa of Ávila. Two years before her death, the pope approved the association's statutes. Two decades later, Pope John Paul II would use those same statutes as the constitutions of what is referred to as the 1990s Discalced Carmelites. These constitutions are virtually identical to those of Saint Teresa of Ávila, which Saint Maravillas worked with faithful love to instill into the heart and soul of every Carmel she established.

Mother Maravillas died on December 11, 1974. She was canonized a saint in 2003 by John Paul II. The miracle that resulted in her canonization is as astounding as she was. A bereaved mother prayed to Maravillas to restore her toddler son to life after a horrible accidental drowning. The child had not breathed in almost a day and had been declared dead by several doctors. This must have touched the motherly heart of Maravillas up in heaven, for by her intercession, the child rose from the dead with no brain damage. Doctors were dumbfounded—but what do you expect from a saint whose very name means "wonders"?

Saint Maravillas would be a good patron saint for mothers who find themselves constantly uprooted by travel or moves, especially military spouses. She would also be a wonderful patroness for mothers who have a hectic schedule, or who find themselves snowed under by many demands upon their time and talents. Finally, she can be a patroness for mothers whose families and communities do not support their vocation.

Prayer from the Roman Missal: Common for Holy Men and Women—for a Nun

O God, who called your handmaid, Saint Maravillas, to seek you before all else, grant that, serving you, through her example and intercession, with a pure and humble heart, we may come at last to your eternal glory. Through our Lord Jesus Christ, your Son, who lives and reigns with you in the unity of the Holy Spirit, God, for ever and ever. Amen.